K. Frazier B.Hoskins R. Na[illegible]

Let's Speak English

Teacher's Book 1

with songs by Carolyn Graham

Oxford University Press

Contents

Introduction	Page 3
Syllabus	Page 8
Unit 1	Page 10
Unit 2	Page 19
Let's Review	Page 28
Unit 3	Page 30
Unit 4	Page 38
Let's Review	Page 46
Unit 5	Page 48
Unit 6	Page 56
Let's Review	Page 65
Unit 7	Page 67
Unit 8	Page 76
Let's Review	Page 85
Midterm and Final Tests	Page 87
Answer Key and Materials Needed	Page 95
Word List	Page 96

Introduction

DESCRIPTION OF THE COURSE

Let's Speak English is a two-level course for junior classes. The themes and situations throughout the books are universal to children everywhere.

Each level has four basic components which are designed to be closely co-ordinated in the classroom: the *Pupil's Book, Workbook, Teacher's Book,* and cassette.

THE PUPIL'S BOOK

The Pupil's Books have a clear and attractive format and are illustrated throughout in full colour. Creative activities, using a wide range of skills, engage pupils in a variety of learning experiences. Pupil's Books 1 and 2 contain eight units, each providing material for from five to seven 50-minute lessons, as well as four review units.

Level One of *Let's Speak English* focuses on the development of basic oral language through functional dialogues, question and answer patterns, and vocabulary work. Language structures covered include the simple present tense of the verbs *to be, to have, to want,* and *to like,* the present continuous tense, plurals, adjectives, and prepositions.

THE WORKBOOK

The Workbook provides reading and writing practice to further reinforce the language introduced in the Pupil's Book.

THE TEACHER'S BOOK

The lessons in the Teacher's Book contain all the components necessary to teach the material in the Pupil's Book in a thorough, organized, and interesting manner. Each easy-to-follow lesson plan describes activities designed to practise and reinforce the new language. These include whole class practice as well as carefully controlled group work and pair work. The plan also contains the tapescript for that lesson and simple instructions for relevant Workbook pages. At the top of each lesson plan are lists of the patterns and vocabulary covered and the materials needed. Duplicatable midterm and final tests, plus an answer key, appear at the back of the Teacher's Book, together with a handy summary of all the materials needed for Level One. On the last page there is a Word List of all the vocabulary presented in the Pupil's Book.

THE CASSETTE

The accompanying cassette contains the dialogues, alphabet letters and sounds, listening tests, and original songs by Carolyn Graham, as well as listening activities for the review units.

TESTING

The testing built into *Let's Speak English* allows the teacher to closely monitor the pupils' progress at regular intervals. In addition to the listening test in each unit, each book contains a midterm and final test.

PHILOSOPHY AND PRINCIPLES

Let's Speak English is a thorough, enjoyable course – emphasizing communication within a carefully controlled grammatical syllabus. Beginning with the first lesson, pupils are provided with a variety of activities focusing on interactive communication which gradually increase in difficulty. Pupils are regularly presented with new vocabulary and structures so that they have adequate language to communicate with at each new level.

Experiences that are familiar to children are featured throughout the course in dialogues, songs, and exercises. This encourages pupils to begin speaking in English about situations they can easily relate to.

The lessons in *Let's Speak English* incorporate techniques from several methods that have repeatedly proved successful in teaching English to children. These include James Asher's Total Physical Response (TPR), which is based, in part, on the belief that linking physical action with language will aid retention; the Functional Approach, which emphasizes the proper context in which to use certain expressions; the Communicative Approach, which is based on the belief that language used in the classroom should be used to communicate thoughts and feelings that are meaningful to the pupils; the Audio-Lingual Approach, which focuses on the sounds and syntax of the language; and Grammar/Structural Approaches, which examine the grammar of the language.

BOOK ONE—ORGANIZATION OF A UNIT

Each of the eight units in the Pupil's Book is organized around a basic theme and is divided into seven sections. Each section is indicated by a colourful icon which tells the teacher and the pupil at a glance the purpose of the lesson. The same icons are used in the Workbook to help the teacher and pupils to identify corresponding pages in both books.

Each unit in the Pupil's Book contains the following sections:

Let's Talk—Functional language is introduced in a dialogue relating to the topic of the unit.

Let's Sing—The functional language introduced in *Let's Talk* is practised in an interactive song.

Let's Learn—In this section, new vocabulary and a new grammatical structure are introduced. The structures are presented in a short, realistic dialogue and are then practised in a variety of activities.

Let's Learn Some More—This section builds on the grammar pattern introduced in *Let's Learn* by presenting a related grammatical structure. A dialogue is again used to demonstrate the language, followed by practice exercises.

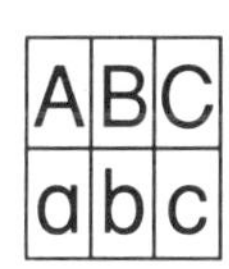

Let's Learn the Alphabet—This section can be used at any time in the unit. In Unit One, the entire alphabet is introduced. The remaining seven units each include three or four letters, together with their sounds as the initial letters of key words.

Let's Move—This section covers classroom commands and action verbs. Pupils follow simple commands and directions and then give commands to fellow classmates.

Let's Listen—This section reviews the language learned in the unit through a variety of listening and interactive activities. The Pupil's Book includes a formal listening test in which pupils select the correct answer from two choices. This can also be done as an in-class review activity.

Let's Review—At the end of every two units, a review unit helps to reinforce previously studied structures and vocabulary. In games, role plays, and interviews, the pupils recycle the material from previous units, further strengthening the base from which they can then move on to more advanced language.

USING THE TEACHER'S BOOK

Review

Every class should begin with an oral review of language already studied. This helps the pupils to remember previous material and starts the class on a positive note, since the pupils are repeating something they have already learned to do.

The Review section of each unit in the Teacher's Book contains varied, engaging activities. These include songs, games, and command reviews.

Presentation

Pupils should be introduced to the new vocabulary and structures before they open their books. The language will thus already be familiar to them when they first see the new structures and vocabulary in written form.

The Presentation section describes, in detail, ways to introduce the new material through the use of puppets or soft toys, realia, simple board drawings, and mime.

Open Your Books

This section explains in detail how to proceed once the pupils have opened their books. It describes how and when to use the cassette, and how to present the sample structures and contractions (which appear in boxes on Pupil's Book pages). The section also describes different ways of practising the material so that pupils can thoroughly absorb it.

Extension

The Extension section describes more game-like activities which recycle the material from the lesson in innovative and enjoyable ways. This is a good way to end a class since the pupils will leave with a sense of accomplishment, wanting to learn more.

TEACHING TECHNIQUES AND PROCEDURES

PRONUNCIATION

In *Let's Speak English* Pupil's Book 1, pronunciation drills and practice do not receive major emphasis. This stems from the belief that it is desirable, especially with younger children, to begin language instruction without placing undue stress on the exact pronunciation of each word or phrase. Too much attention to this can result in pupil frustration, lack of confidence, and lack of interest in the language. Most important at the first stage is to develop a degree of ease in communicating in the new language, and a desire to speak it without having to worry about making errors in pronunciation at every step. This is crucial for pupils' motivation, without which they will not learn the language.

The lessons in the Teacher's Book do, however, incorporate some pronunciation practice at each stage. This is done through choral repetition and further oral practice in pairs. During this time, the teacher should circulate around the classroom, listening to the pupils and helping those who are having trouble.

Let's Speak English stresses natural speech through the contraction examples which accompany the sample structure boxes. Pupils are given many opportunities to practise both the full and contracted forms of words, thus increasing their fluency and naturalness in speaking.

GROUPING THE STUDENTS FOR LANGUAGE PRACTICE

Varying the way in which new structures are practised helps to keep the pupils interested in the language. After modelling a new structure, have the whole class repeat it. If the language is complicated, or there are more than one or two items being introduced, it can be practised in a drill. Keep the drill moving to maintain the pupils' attention. After the whole class has practised the new structure, divide the class into two groups to practise again, this time with each group taking a part of the dialogue or pattern. Practising in two groups allows the pupils to become more familiar with the patterns within the secure setting of speaking to other pupils.

The pupils can then be placed in pairs for further practice. This is an ideal way for pupils to learn from each other, since they can share information and ask questions about points they are unsure of. The teacher should closely monitor the pairs by walking round the classroom and helping as needed. Only after adequate whole-class and group practice should pupils be asked to speak in front of the class. (The latter should be done more as a game or role play than as a method of testing.)

MODELLING

Clear, careful modelling is essential to demonstrate the procedure for certain activities. Good modelling saves time later and helps the pupils get the most out of an activity linguistically, since they will not be wasting energy in confusion about what they should be doing. Finally, and most important, modelling enables the teacher to explain a structure or activity, and the pupils to carry out the activity, using only English.

All new sentence patterns, dialogues, and practice activities should be modelled. This can be done in several ways. The teacher can act as two people, or use puppets or soft toys to demonstrate a new question and answer pattern. Realia should be used whenever possible, along with appropriate gestures.

Teacher: *What's this?* (Holding up a book.)
It's a book.

VOCABULARY

Realia, magazine pictures, and simple board drawings can be used to present new words. One method is the following: Hold up an object or picture and say the word. Ask the pupils to repeat the word three times. Then practise the word with drills using language the pupils are already familiar with. The Teacher's Book describes a number of drills and activities designed to develop and reinforce vocabulary.

There are two types of vocabulary or language that all learners develop—receptive language and productive language. Receptive language is the language pupils understand but are not necessarily able to produce yet. Productive language is the language pupils use when they speak. When the teacher speaks to the pupils in English it is inevitable that he or she will sometimes use language that the pupils have not yet studied. This is not a problem and is even desirable, since it exposes the pupils to additional language. They will gradually pick up the meaning from the context if the language is used often enough.

Receptive language can be practised by getting pupils to recognize and physically respond to news words. For example, put a book and a pencil on the board rail or on a table at the front of the classroom. Say *book* and ask the class (or a group or one pupil) to point to the book.

Productive language practice requires the pupils to say the words as they identify the objects. Do the activity just mentioned and ask pupils to touch the correct objects, as well as orally identify them.

COMMANDS AND ACTION SENTENCES

To introduce new commands (or action sentences), the following procedure is recommended. First, say a command, such as *Open your books,* and then demonstrate it by opening your book. Next, say the command and ask the whole class to do or mime the action. Say the command again and ask the pupils to repeat the command and do or mime the action. Using this approach will give the pupils time to understand the meaning of the command first (receptive language); they will then feel confident about saying it aloud (productive language).

After the commands have been introduced, quickly practise them as a whole class and then in two groups. Give half the class a command to do and then give a command to the other half. Alternate between the groups, keeping the practice lively and moving. Finally, put the pupils into pairs to practise the commands and have them give the commands to each other.

Commands in the real world are often used in a sequence (in giving directions, for example). It is, therefore, a good idea to practise command chains with the pupils. Command chains are two or more commands that are linked together: *Open your bag. Take out your book.* These command chains can be practised as a whole class or in two or more groups. Pupils should wait to do or mime the commands until two or more commands have been given. The number of commands in the chain can gradually be increased so that pupils will have to remember longer and longer chunks of language.

In addition to practising the commands and action verbs as they are in the book, vary them by using the verbs with different vocabulary words the class has learned. For example: *Open your bag, open the door, pick up your book,* etc. Give varied commands and have the pupils do or mime the actions. Try to review vocabulary with the commands whenever possible in the review section at the beginning of a class.

Greetings and other functional language can also be combined with the commands.

T: *Hello, (David). How are you?*
David: *I'm fine, thank you.*
T: *David, please go to the board. Write your name.*

Such practice gives the pupils a chance to review language studied in other lessons. In addition, they will begin to see that English fits together in a variety of ways.

It is also good for the pupils to have an opportunity to take the teacher role and give commands to the class, since this will help keep the classroom pupil-centred.

PHONICS

In Level One, *Let's Speak English* introduces the pupils to phonics, or sound and letter association, by focusing on the letters of the alphabet in the initial position of key words. The cassette contains each letter of the alphabet with its sound pronounced, as well as a word beginning with this letter.

Procedurally, the teacher should point to each letter in the book and say it three times, with the pupils repeating each time. Then show the key word and its picture. Emphasize the initial letter when saying the word. Get the pupils to practise printing both the big and small letter after practice in recognizing the letters. Additional pages at the front of the Workbook provide guided practice in printing both capital and small letters.

READING

Words are printed in the text so that the pupils are exposed to them; however, pupils are not expected to be able to decode every vocabulary word in Level One by the end of the book. The focus is on developing the pupils' oral skills. Pupils are, however, expected to be able to recognize and print the entire alphabet, read basic words (including *a, the, I, am, he, she, it, is, they, are, what,* and *this),* to recognize the numbers in both numeral and word form, and put words and sentences in correct order.

WRITING

Written exercises for Level One of *Let's Speak English* are in the accompanying Workbook. Pupils practise letter recognition in a variety of exercises. They also practise printing the letters in tracing exercises which gradually guide them to print entire words and sentences on their own. These exercises can be done in class or at home; however, if the Workbook is to be done at home, it is advisable to spend some class time showing the pupils how to do the exercises. (In Units 1–7 there is an additional Workbook page for the Let's Learn and Let's Learn Some More sections, containing exercises that are slightly more demanding. In Unit 8 there are extra Workbook pages for Let's Learn and Let's Move.)

DRILLS AND GAMES

DRILLS

Drilling is a time-efficient, enjoyable way to recycle material in a tightly organized manner. The material can be from previous lessons, in which case the drill is more of a review; or it can be from the current lesson, in which case the drill can form an integral part of the presentation.

When doing drills, it is a good idea to alternate between choral and individual responses. When doing the latter, choosing pupils in random order and maintaining a quick pace will help prevent the pupils' attention from wandering.

A brief description of several kinds of drills and the procedures for doing them appears below.

Repetition Drill

Model vocabulary words or new language patterns for the class to repeat.

T: *a dog, a dog*
Ps: *a dog*
T: *a rabbit, a rabbit*
Ps: *a rabbit*

or:

T: *This is a red book.*
Ps: *This is a red book.*
T: *This is a yellow pencil.*
Ps: *This is a yellow pencil.*

Substitution Drill

To do a substitution drill, use realia or pictures as cues.

T: *Where are the books?* (Shows a picture of books on a table.) *They're on the table.*
Ps: *They're on the table.*
T: (Shows a picture of books under a table.)
Ps: *They're under the table.*

or:

T: (Shows a picture of a bird.) *There's a bird. I like birds.*
Ps: *There's a bird. I like birds.*
T: (Shows a picture of a frog.)
Ps: *There's a frog. I like frogs.*

Chain Drill

In a chain drill, the teacher should use realia or pictures as cues where these are needed. Show an object to the first pupil and ask a related question. The pupil answers and turns to the next pupil to ask the same question with appropriate substitutions. Continue until all the pupils have had a chance to ask and answer the question.

T: (Shows a picture of a robot.) *What's this?*
P1: *It's a robot.* (P1 shows a picture of a skipping rope.) *What's this?*
P2: *It's a skipping rope.*

NOTE: Chain drills can also be used to practise dialogues (such as greetings) where no cues are needed.
T: *Hello. My name is (Miss Lee). What's your name?*
P1: *My name is(Kate).* To P2: *What's your name?*

Conversation Lines

Pupils stand in two parallel lines facing each other. Each facing pair asks and answers the question and answer pattern or dialogue being practised. Then the two lines move in opposite directions, one to the left and one to the right, so that every pupil has a new partner opposite. The teacher should walk behind the lines, helping pupils as necessary.

GAMES

Beanbag Game

Pupils stand in a circle or remain seated. Toss a beanbag or a ball to one pupil and ask a question (for example, *What's your name?*). P1 responds, tosses the beanbag to another pupil, and repeats the question. Continue around and across the circle until all pupils have had a turn. (Note that pupils should not toss the beanbag to pupils on either side of them.)

Bingo

Each pupil has a nine-square grid, three rows of three squares each. These can be made by the teacher or by the pupils themselves. Each pupil fills in the squares with drawings, numbers, letters, or colours, or a few of each—choosing from a selection provided by the teacher. When the teacher or a pupil volunteer calls out the name of an object or a colour, letter, or number, the pupils who have those on their grids cross them out. The winner is the first pupil to cover three squares across, down, or diagonally.

Charades

Pupils act out commands, action verbs, adjectives, prepositions, etc without speaking. The class must guess the command. If cues are needed, the actor(s) can look in the Pupil's Book or the teacher can whisper instructions.

Find Your Partners

Prepare slips of coloured paper. There should be several of each colour—ideally in multiples corresponding to the number of lines in the pattern to be practised. Give each pupil a slip and say the name of a colour—for example, *Red.* All pupils with red slips stand up and practise the dialogue.

Guessing Game

The teacher, or a pupil volunteer, thinks of an object. The other pupils must guess what it is by asking questions. Then the whole class describes the object in a full sentence. For example:

P1: *Is it (big)?*
T: *(No, it isn't.)*
P2: *Is it (little)?*
T: *(Yes, it is.)*
P3: *Is it (a robot)?*
T: *(Yes, it is.)*
Ps: *It's a (little) (robot).*

(Alternative: Divide class into two groups. All pupils in Group A quickly draw pictures containing several objects of their choice from list of words being studied. Then each Group A pupil, in turn, tells Group B counterpart what is in her/his picture. Group B pupils draw pictures following descriptions and results are compared. Then reverse roles.)

Living Sentences or Dialogues

Select sentences from the present unit or a previous one. Divide the pupils into groups and assign one sentence to each group. Each pupil in the group is then assigned one word in the sentence. Pupils are not allowed to speak except to repeat their words. They arrange themselves in the correct order. For dialogues, pupils are assigned sentences rather than words.

Memory Chain

Divide the class into two or three teams. In turn, each team tries to make the chain as long as possible, without forgetting any items. Award points for the longest chain. Each pupil adds one item to the chain. For example:

P1: *I like (rabbits).*
P2: *I like (rabbits) and (dogs).*
P3: *I like (rabbits) and (dogs) and (frogs).*

Number Grids

Give each pupil a grid with three or more numbered squares. The pupil draws an object in each square (using pictures in the Pupil's Book as cues if necessary). Then they describe their drawings in a chain drill. For example, pupils draw animals. The teacher starts the game by giving the first number.

T: *Number 1.*
P1 (Looks at own drawing): *There's (a dog) in number 1.*
P2 (Looks at own drawing): *Yes, there is* or *No, there isn't. There's a (cat) in number 1.*

Pass the Puppet

Play a song from the cassette (or any other music) while the pupils quickly pass a puppet, toy, or other object to each other. When the music stops the class asks the pupil who is holding the puppet a question. The pupil answers and the music is started again.

Picture Dictation

Pupils draw simple pictures in response to instructions from the teacher or a pupil volunteer. Then they compare pictures. This can also be done in two groups: each pupil, in turn, gives instructions to a pupil in the other group.

Please

In small groups, pupils are given commands from the present and previous units. If the teacher says *Please* in front of the command, pupils should do or mime the action. If the teacher does not say *Please,* pupils should remain still.

The Right Choice

Divide the class into two teams. Put two or more objects or coloured squares on the board rail or table. Or draw objects on the board. One pupil from each team in turn comes up to the front. The teacher names an object or a colour and the pupil picks it up or points to it. If the choice is correct, the team wins a point.

Tic Tac Toe

Draw a numbered nine-square grid on the board. Divide the class into two teams and assign the symbol X to one team and O to the other. Ask a pupil from Team A a question. If the pupil answers correctly, he or she can place an X or O on the grid in the location of their choice which they can indicate by stating the number. The first team to earn three Xs or Os in a row on the grid wins. (Instead of asking a question, the teacher can make a statement about one of several objects on the board rail/table or one of several drawings. A correct choice earns an X or an O.)

Treasure Hunt

Divide the class into pairs (or play the game as a whole-class activity). Give the class a verbal list of objects to 'find' in the classroom (for example, a red book, a yellow pencil, etc.). Keep the list short enough to be remembered (three or four objects). Each pair must 'hunt' for these objects by looking round the classroom while remaining seated. When they have found all the objects, they put their hands up. When all pairs are ready, ask pupil volunteers to tell the class the location of each object (or to stand by the object). The class repeats the location in a full sentence. Ps: *The red book is under the desk. The yellow pencil is on the chair.,* etc.

Whispering Game

Divide the class into two groups. Whisper a sentence to the first pupil in one group. (Or ask a question out loud and whisper a reply.) That pupil whispers what she/he heard to the next pupil and so on. When the last pupil has heard the sentence she/he stands up and says it. Then the first pupil repeats the original sentence and the two are compared.

Syllabus

UNIT	LANGUAGE ITEMS	FUNCTIONS	TOPICS
1	Hello, I am (Andy). Hi! My name is (Kate). What's your name? What's this? It's (a book). Is this (a book)? Yes, it is. No, it isn't.	Greetings Introducing yourself Asking someone's name Asking about objects (singular) Identifying objects (singular) Classroom commands	Names Classroom objects
2	How are you? I'm fine, thank you. What colour is it? It's (red). This is a (blue) (book). This is a (red) and (yellow) book.	Greetings Asking about colours Identifying colours Describing objects Classroom commands	Colours Classroom objects
3	This is my friend, (Sarah). Hello, (Sarah). Let's play. What are these? They're (cassettes). How many (trainers)? (Ten) (trainers).	Introducing friends Suggesting an activity Asking about objects (plural) Identifying objects (plural) Asking about numbers Counting 1–10 Classroom commands	Numbers 1–10 Classroom objects
4	Hi, Mum! I'm home. This is my (mother). It's nice to meet you. It's nice to meet you, too. Who's (she)? (She's) my (grandmother). (She's) (short). Don't (watch TV).	Introducing family members Meeting someone politely Asking about people Identifying people Describing people Negative commands	Family
5	Happy birthday, (Jenny)! How old are you? I'm (seven) years old. This is for you. It's (my) birthday today. What is it? I don't know. It's (little). It's a (little) (yo-yo). Can you (play with a yo-yo)? Yes, I can. No, I can't.	Birthday greetings Asking and telling age Giving a gift Guessing Describing objects Asking about ability	Birthdays Age Toys

UNIT	LANGUAGE ITEMS	FUNCTIONS	TOPICS
6	Is the (sun) (shining)? Is the (sun) (shining) now? No, it's (raining). The (sun) is (shining). How many (clouds) are there? There are (six) (clouds). There's one (cloud). Where's the (kite)? It's (in) the tree. Where are the (books)? They're (under) the (table). I'm (climbing a tree). Is he (climbing a tree)?	Asking about the weather Describing the weather Counting Describing a situation Asking about location Specifying location Asking about ability	Weather Outdoor activities
7	I'm (hungry). I want (an apple). Here you are. Thank you. You're welcome. What do you want? I want (some cake) and (some ice cream). Do you want (some chicken)? Yes, I do. No, I don't. I'm (buying) (an apple). I'm (washing) it.	Expressing hunger and thirst Asking what someone wants Expressing wants Logical sequencing	Food and drink
8	What's your favourite colour? (Red) What do you like? I like (blue). I like (frogs). I like (frogs), too Do you like (spiders)? Yes, I do. No, I don't. I'm (walking). Can it (swim)? Yes, it can. No, it can't.	Asking about favourites Expressing likes Agreeing Asking about ability	Favourite colours Animals

Unit One

Let's Talk

LANGUAGE PATTERNS: Hello, I am (Andy). What's your name? My name is (John).

NEW VOCABULARY: Hello, Hi, name. Pupils' and teacher's names

MATERIALS: name tags or name cards; two puppets or soft toys; tape-recorder and cassette; beanbag or ball

Greet pupils in English as they arrive. Call roll at beginning of first class to be sure of pupils' names. Ask each pupil to write his or her name on a name tag or card.

PRESENTATION

1. Introduce greeting.
a. Introduce yourself to class in English. (Use a wave or handshake to indicate *Hello.*)

T: *Hello. I am (Miss Lee).*

b. Greet every pupil by name.

T: *Hello, (Kate).*

c. Say each pupil's name in turn. Pupil indicates his/her presence by putting hand up. Ask class to turn towards pupil, wave, and say greeting.

T: *(Tommy)*
Ps: *Hello, (Tommy).*

Repeat quickly for all pupils.

2. Present first part of dialogue.
a. Use puppets to model first part of dialogue.

Puppet A: *Hello, I am (Kate).*
Puppet B: *Hi! My name is (John).*

b. Pupils repeat each line of the dialogue three times, in chorus.

3. Practise.
a. Divide class into two groups and practise dialogue, using puppets' names.

Group A: *Hello, I am (Kate).*
Group B: *Hi! My name is (John).*

b. Start a **Chain Drill** (see page 6) around the class. Pupils say greeting using own names. Keep drill moving fast.

T to P1: *Hello, I am (Miss Lee).*
P1 to T: *Hi! My name is (Tommy).*
(Then P1 to P2, etc.)

4. Present second part of dialogue.
a. Use puppets to model second part of dialogue.

Puppet A: *What's your name?*
Puppet B: *My name is (Kate).*

Pupils repeat dialogue three times, in chorus.
b. Ask class *What is your name?* All pupils answer together, using own names.

5. Practise.
a. Do a whole class practice. Repeat each line three times. Pupils use own names.

T: *What's your name?*
Ps: *What's your name?*
T: *My name is (Miss Lee).*
Ps: *My name is (Jenny).*

b. In pairs, pupils practise question and answer pattern, using own names. Teacher should circulate, helping pupils as necessary.

OPEN YOUR BOOKS

Open your Pupil's Book to page 6 and show it to pupils. Point to picture. T: *Look at the picture. This is Andy. This is Kate. This is John. They are at school.* Write number 6 on board and point to it. T: *Open your books to page 6.* (Use gestures to indicate open.)

1. Pupils open their books to page 6.
a. Play cassette. Pupils listen and point to character who is speaking.

Andy: *Hello, I am Andy.*
Kate: *Hi! My name is Kate. What's your name?*
John: *My name is John.*

b. Play cassette again, stopping after each line. Pupils repeat line.

2. Present sample structures and contraction.
a. Write structures on board. Read them aloud, pointing to words. Pupils repeat.
b. Write explanation of contraction on board: *What is = What's.* Pupils practise *What is your name?* and *What's your name?* Point to explanation on board as you practise.

3. Practise.
Role-play conversation, using contracted form. Ask three pupil volunteers to come to front of class and model conversation, using own names. Each volunteer should play each part. Then divide class into groups of three and continue.

EXTENSION

1. Beanbag Game (see page 6). Pupils stand in a circle (or remain seated). Toss a beanbag or ball to P1 and ask P1's name. T: *What's your name?* P1 answers, using own name: *My name is (Kate).* P1 then tosses beanbag to another pupil and asks P2's name. Continue.

WORKBOOK page 9

- Pupils name characters and trace strings from children's hands to balloons. Then they trace words in speech bubbles. Then they practise question and answer pattern.
- Pupils write own names in blank at bottom of page.

Let's Sing

LANGUAGE PATTERNS: Hello/Hi. What's your name? My name is (John). Hello, (John).

NEW VOCABULARY: names of *Let's Speak English* characters (John, Scott, Andy, Lisa, Kate, Jenny)

MATERIALS: two puppets or soft toys; tape-recorder and cassette

REVIEW

In pairs, pupils greet each other. Teacher should circulate, helping as necessary.

P1: *Hello, I am (Kate).*
P2: *Hi! My name is (John).*

PRESENTATION

1. Review question and answer.
a. Use puppets to model question and answer.

Puppet A: *What's your name?*
Puppet B: *My name is (Kate).*

b. Pupils repeat each line of dialogue three times, in chorus.

2. Practise.
a. Divide class into two groups and practise question and answer pattern. Pupils use own names.

Group A: *What's your name?*
Group B: *My name is (Kate).*

Then reverse roles.
b. Do a **Chain Drill** (see page 6).

P1: *My name is (Jack).* To P2: *What's your name?*
P2: *My name is (Jill).* To P3: *What's your name?*

3. Combine greeting and question.
a. Use puppets to model dialogue.

Puppet A: *Hello. My name is (John). What's your name?*
Puppet B: *Hi! My name is (Kate).*

b. Pupils practise in two groups, using own names.

4. Practise.
Conversation Lines (see page 6).
Pupils stand in two parallel lines facing each other. Each pupil greets the pupil standing opposite and the two pupils ask each other their names. Then the two lines move in opposite directions, one to the left and one to the right, so that every pupil has a new partner. Teacher should walk behind lines, helping pupils as necessary.
(Alternative: Select random pairs to practise dialogue, in turn, seated.)

OPEN YOUR BOOKS

Open your Pupil's Book to page 7 and show it to pupils. Point to the characters and name them. Pupils repeat each name.

1. Pupils open their books to page 7.
a. Play cassette. Pupils listen and point to John when they hear his name. Stop cassette after verse 1.

Hello, hello, hello!
What's your name?
Hello, hello, hello!

My name is John.
My name is John.

Hello John!
Hello John!
Hello!

b. Play verse 1 again. Pupils sing along.
c. Remind pupils of characters' names. Then play rest of song. Pupils point to each character as they hear the name.
d. Play entire song once more. Pupils sing along.

2. Practise.
Sing the song in two groups.

Group A: *Hello, hello, hello.*
What's your name?
Hello, hello, hello.
Group B: *My name is John. My name is John.*
All: *Hello John! Hello John!*
Hello.

Reverse roles and sing again.

EXTENSION

1. Sing 'The Hello Song', with pupils using their own names. Sing several times, pointing to individual pupils: pupil then sings *My name is (John).*

2. Pass the Puppet (see page 7). Play song from cassette or any other music as pupils pass puppet around. When music stops, class says: *Hello. What's your name?* Pupil holding puppet answers using own name. P1: *My name is (John).* Ps: *Hello (John)!*

Let's Learn

LANGUAGE PATTERNS: What's this? It's (a bag).

NEW VOCABULARY: ruler, pencil, book, desk, chair, pen, bag, eraser

MATERIALS: classroom objects (as listed above); cloth; two puppets or soft toys; tape-recorder and cassette; bag

REVIEW

1. Conversation Lines (see page 6). Pupils practise *What's your name? My name is (John),* using own names.

PRESENTATION

1. Present new vocabulary.

a. Use realia to introduce new words one at a time.

T: *A ruler, a ruler.*
Ps: *A ruler.*

Pupils repeat each word several times.

b. Quickly pass objects round the class, one at a time, to practise new words. Each pupil says name of object as he/she passes it.

c. Give each pupil an object. Say name of one object. Whole class repeats name and pupil holding object holds it up. Continue for all objects.

2. Present pattern.

a. Partially hide an object under a cloth. Use puppets to model question and answer.

Puppet A: *What's this?*
Puppet B: *It's (a bag).*

b. Pupils repeat each line of dialogue three times, in chorus.

c. Hide or quickly show other objects to pupils and ask *What's this?* Pupils answer as in model. Continue for all new words.

3. Practise.
Divide class into two groups. Give classroom objects to Group A. Each pupil in Group A takes a turn to show one object to Group B.

P1 in Group A: *What's this?*
Group B: *It's (an eraser).*

After Group A finishes, pupils in Group B ask Group A the questions.

OPEN YOUR BOOKS

Open your Pupil's Book to page 8. Point to the characters and ask pupils to name them. Point to half-hidden ruler.

T: *What's this? It's a ruler.*

1. Pupils open their books to page 8.

a. Play cassette. Pupils listen and point to ruler and cat respectively.

Jenny: *What's this?*
Scott: *It's a ruler.*
John: *What's this? It's a cat!*

b. Play cassette again, stopping after each line. Pupils repeat line.

2. Present sample structures and contractions.

a. Write sample structures on board. Read them aloud, pointing to words. Pupils repeat.

b. Write explanation of contractions on board:
What is = What's
It is = It's.

c. Pupils practise *What is this?, What's this?, It is a cat,* and *It's a cat.* Point to explanation on board as you practise.

3. Practise.

a. Divide class into two groups. Practise question and answer pattern with new vocabulary on PB page 9, using two cats as models. One group is the Black Cat and the other is the Orange Cat. Then reverse roles.

Black Cat: *What's this?*
Orange Cat: *It's (a book).*

Give special practice to *It's an eraser.*

b. In pairs, pupils continue asking and answering questions about pictures on page 9.

EXTENSION

1. Tic Tac Toe (see page 7). Divide class into two teams, X and O. Draw a numbered nine-square grid on board. Put classroom objects on board rail. One pupil from each team, in turn, comes up to board and teacher makes a statement about an object. T: *It's (a pen).* If pupil picks up correct object, he/she can place an X or O in grid.

2. Put one classroom object from lesson into a bag. One pupil holds bag up to class and pulls out object.

P1: *What's this?*
All: *It's (a pencil).*

Continue with all objects. Let as many pupils as possible ask the question.

(Continued on page 13.)

WORKBOOK pages 10 and 11

page 10

- Pupils trace names of classroom objects.
- Pupils trace words. Then they practise question and answer pattern.
- Pupils draw picture of classroom object of their choice and write its name to complete sentence.

page 11

- Pupils trace words. Then they draw a line from each sentence to matching picture.
- Pupils draw lines from full forms to matching contractions. (**Answers:** *It is — It's / What is — What's.)* Then they trace words.
- Pupils draw a line from each question to matching answer. (**Answers:** *What's your name? My name's Kate. / What's this? It's a book.)*

Let's Learn Some More

LANGUAGE PATTERNS: Is this (an eraser)? Yes, it is. No, it isn't.

VOCABULARY: Review of classroom objects

MATERIALS: classroom objects for Let's Learn vocabulary; two puppets or soft toys; tape-recorder and cassette

REVIEW

1. Greet class. Pupils reply, using own names.

T: *Hello. My name is (Miss Lee). What's your name?*
Ps: *Hi! My name is (Jane).*

Then pupils greet each other in pairs.

2. Use realia to review classroom object vocabulary.

T: *What's this?*
Ps: *It's (a pencil).*

PRESENTATION

1. Present pattern.
a. Use puppets to model question and affirmative answer pattern.

Puppet A: *What's this?* (Points to a book.)
Puppet B: *It's a book.*
Puppet A: *Is this a book?* (Points to another book.)
Puppet B: *Yes, it is.*

b. Pupils repeat each line of dialogue three times, in chorus.

2. Practise question and affirmative answer pattern, using realia for Let's Learn vocabulary.
a. Hold up each object in turn.

T: *Is this (a book)?*
Ps: *Yes, it is.*

b. Divide class into two groups. Repeat practice, with each group taking time to ask and answer questions. Use realia to cue groups.
c. Repeat practice in pairs. Teacher should circulate, helping as necessary.

3. Present next part of pattern.
a. Use puppets to model question and negative answer pattern.

Puppet A: *Is this a book?* (Points to an eraser.)
Puppet B: *No, it isn't. It's an eraser.*

b. Pupils repeat each line of dialogue three times, in chorus.

4. Practise question and negative answer pattern, using realia for Let's Learn vocabulary.
a. Hold up each object in turn and use incorrect name in question.

T: *Is this (a book)?*
Ps: *No, it isn't. It's (an eraser).*

b. Repeat practice in two groups.
c. Repeat practice in pairs. Teacher should circulate, helping as necessary.

OPEN YOUR BOOKS

Open your Pupil's Book to page 10. Point to picture. T: *Look at the pictures. This is a classroom. This is the teacher. These are the pupils.*

1. Pupils open their books to page 10.
a. Play cassette. Pupils listen and point to objects.

Teacher: *Is this a book?*
All: *Yes, it is.*
Teacher: *Is this a desk?*
All: *No, it isn't. It's a chair.*

b. Play cassette again, stopping after each line. Pupils repeat line.

2. Present sample structures and contraction.
a. Write structures on board. Read them aloud, pointing to words. Pupils repeat.
b. Write explanation of contraction on board: *is not = isn't.*
c. Pupils practise *No, it is not* and *No, it isn't.* Point to explanation on board as you practise.

3. Practise.
Look at activity at top of PB page 11.
a. Model question and answer pattern presented by cats. Pupils repeat.
b. Divide class into two groups. Groups take turns to answer questions about each of the pictures, in order.

T: *Is this (a pen)?*
Group A: *Yes, it is* or *No, it isn't. It's (a pencil).*

EXTENSION

1. Divide class into two teams, Black Cats and Orange Cats. On the board, draw a game board like the one on PB page 11. Ask Black Cats *Is this (a pen)?* using classroom object as cue. If they answer correctly, give them one point. Alternate questions between teams. Continue until questions have been asked about all objects.

(Continued on page 15.)

WORKBOOK pages 12 and 13

page 12

- Pupils circle correct answers. (**Answers**: *No, it is not. No, it is not. Yes, it is.*) Then they practise question and answer pattern.
- Pupils trace words to complete answers.

page 13

- Pupils trace words. Then they draw lines from full forms to matching contractions. (**Answers**: *is not — isn't / it is — it's / what is — what's)*
- Pupils complete questions to match answers. (**Answers**: *What's your name? What's this? Is this a pencil? Is this a book?)* Then they trace words.
- Pupils complete each pair of sentences in dialogue. (**Answers**: *Hello. My name is Jenny* or *I'm Jenny. Hi! My name is Lisa* or *I'm Lisa. / What's your name? My name is Andy. / What's this? It's a bag. / Is this an eraser? No, it isn't. / Is this a pencil? Yes, it is.*) Then they trace words.

Let's Learn the Alphabet

NEW VOCABULARY: alphabet

MATERIALS: tape-recorder and cassette

1. Write whole alphabet, in capital letters, on board.

2. Introduce alphabet in sections like *A-B-C* or *A-B-C-D-E-F-G*. Sections of no more than seven letters are recommended. (For young classes, no more than three to five letters.) Point to the letters as you say them. Pupils repeat each letter.

3. Pupils open their books to bottom of page 11. Play 'The Alphabet Song' on cassette.

A B ABC
A B C D EFG
A B C D E F G H I like English!

A B ABC
A B C D EFG
H I J K
L M N O I like English!

A B ABC
A B C D EFG

H I J K
L M N O
P Q R S T Wow!

I like English!
I like English!

A B C D EFG
H I J K L M N O

P Q R S TUV
W X Y Z I like English!

4. Play cassette again. Pupils sing along, pointing to letters.

5. Repeat song (with or without the cassette). Pupils move in rhythm to song.

WORKBOOK page 14

- Pupils trace short dotted lines. Then they join letters in alphabetical order (twice).

Let's Move

LANGUAGE PATTERNS: stand up, sit down, open your book, close your book, please be quiet, listen carefully, point to the teacher, touch the desk

VOCABULARY: Unit review

MATERIALS: classroom objects for Let's Learn vocabulary; cloth; tape-recorder and cassette

REVIEW

1. Divide class into two groups and sing 'The Hello Song'. Group A should sing the greeting and Group B should represent John, Kate, and Andy, in turn. Then reverse roles, with Group A representing Jenny, Lisa, and Scott. (Alternative: Ask for six pupil volunteers to sing solo responses, using own names.)

2. Question and answer pattern review.
a. Using realia, do quick class review of Let's Learn classroom object vocabulary.

T: *What's this?*
Ps: *It's (an eraser).*

b. Hide classroom objects, one by one, under a cloth. Pupils must guess identity of each object by its shape.

T: *Is this (a pen)?*
Ps: *Yes, it is. / No, it isn't. It's (an eraser).*

PRESENTATION

1. Present commands.
a. Model command phrases in pairs, using clear gestures.

T: *Stand up. Sit down.* (Repeat and model several times.)

b. Say commands. Pupils listen and do commands.
c. Repeat commands. Pupils listen, repeat, and do commands.
d. Divide class into two groups. Give a pair of commands to one group at a time. Group does and says commands.

2. Play a game.
Divide class into teams. Give a pair of commands to one pupil on each team. If action is done correctly, award team point.

OPEN YOUR BOOKS

Open your Pupil's Book to page 12 and show it to pupils. Point to each picture in turn and say command. Pupils repeat and do command.

1. Pupils open their books to page 12.
a. Play cassette. Pupils listen and point to each action.

Stand up.
Sit down.
Open your book.
Close your book.
Point to the teacher.
Touch the desk.
Please be quiet.
Listen carefully.

b. Play cassette again, stopping after each command. Pupils say command.

2. Say commands in random order. Pupils repeat and do commands.

3. Each pupil, in turn, points to a picture and gives command (with teacher's help). Class repeats command and does action.

EXTENSION

1. Charades (see page 6). Play charades using command phrases. One pupil at a time chooses a command and acts it out. Class must guess command.

2. Practise a variation on the commands. Use Let's Learn vocabulary in commands. Model for pupils and practise as a class, in groups, and in pairs.

T: *Open your (bag). Close your (bag). Point to the (ruler). Touch the (ruler).*

WORKBOOK page 15

- Pupils trace words and say commands.
- Pupils draw a line from each picture to matching command. Then they trace words.

Let's Listen

LANGUAGE PATTERNS: Unit review

VOCABULARY: Unit review

MATERIALS: classroom objects or magazine pictures for Let's Learn vocabulary; small bag; tape-recorder and cassette

REVIEW

1. Let's Talk.
a. In pairs, pupils practise greetings from Let's Talk and Let's Sing.
b. Role plays. Three pupil volunteers come to front of class and act out dialogue, using own names. Repeat with several other groups of three.

2. Let's Learn.
Give each pupil object/picture for Let's Learn vocabulary. In turn, pupils introduce themselves to class and ask *What's this?*

P1: *Hello. My name is (Sue).*
Ps: *Hi, (Sue).*
P1: *What's this?*
Ps: *It's (a ruler).*

3. Let's Learn Some More.
Ask one pupil to come to front of class and place object in bag while rest of class closes eyes. Pupil then selects another pupil to come up and guess what the object is by feeling it. Repeat with other pupils.

P1: *Is this (a pen)?*
P2: *Yes, it is* or *No, it isn't. It's (a ruler).*

4. Let's Move.
a. Give pupils two commands to perform in sequence. Make sure they listen to both commands before they act them out.

T: *Open your book. Stand up.*

After doing this several times, increase to three commands.
b. Ask volunteer pupils to give commands to class. Teacher helps if necessary.

PRESENTATION

Teach pupils how to do test. Put two classroom objects on board rail. Ask one pupil to stand next to board. Make a statement about one of the objects.

T: *It's (a book).*

Pupil chooses correct object and teacher ticks board above object. Repeat several times until pupils understand procedure.

NOTE: If you want to conduct this as a formal test, go immediately to Step **1b** in Open Your Books.

OPEN YOUR BOOKS

1. Pupils open their books to page 13.
a. Play cassette. Pupils listen and point to correct picture.

1. *It's a pencil.*
2. *It's a desk.*
3. *What's this?*
   It's an eraser.
4. *What's this?*
   It's a bag.
5. *Is this a ruler?*
   Yes, it is.
6. *Is this a chair?*
   No, it isn't. It's a desk.
7. *Point to the book.*
8. *Please be quiet.*

b. Play cassette again. Each pupil does exercise as a written test.

2. Correct tests with pupils.

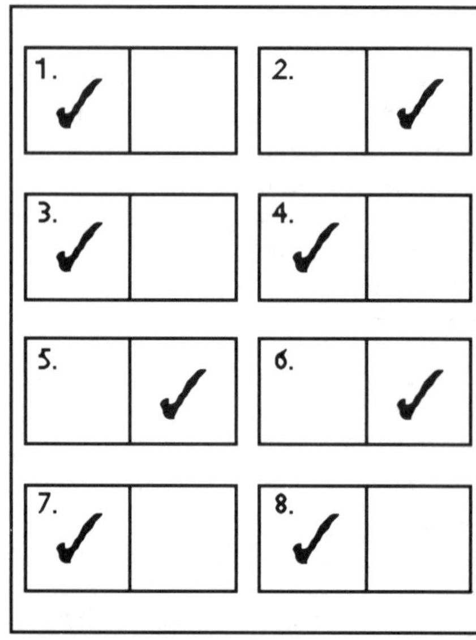

EXTENSION

1. Charades (see page 6). Pairs of pupils act out Let's Move commands (using pictures on PB page 12 as cues if necessary). Class must guess commands.

WORKBOOK page 16

- Pupils circle correct label next to each picture. Then they trace dotted words.
- Pupils circle correct label and write name of object in sentence. (**Answer**: *It is a bag.*)
- Pupils trace words.
- Pupils write answer to question. (**Answer**: *Yes, it is.*) Then they practise all question and answer patterns on page.

Unit Two

Let's Talk

LANGUAGE PATTERNS: Hi, (Andy). How are you? I'm fine, thank you.

VOCABULARY: Review of Unit 1 commands and pupils' names

MATERIALS: two puppets or soft toys; tape-recorder and cassette; beanbag or ball

REVIEW

1. With whole class, quickly practise Unit 1 commands.

2. In pairs, pupils greet each other using Unit 1 dialogue.

PRESENTATION

1. Present first part of dialogue.
a. Use puppets to model basic greeting.

Puppet A: *Hi! How are you?*
Puppet B: *I'm fine, thank you.*

b. Pupils repeat each line of dialogue three times, in chorus.

2. Practise.
a. Divide class into two groups and practise dialogue.

Group A: *Hi! How are you?*
Group B: *I'm fine, thank you.*

b. Do a **Chain Drill** around the class (see page 6). Pupils use own names.

P1: *Hi, (Joe). How are you?*
P2: *I'm fine, thank you.* Turns to P3 *Hi, (Jill). How are you?*
P3: *I'm fine, thank you.*

3. Present complete dialogue.
a. Use puppets to model dialogue.

Puppet A: *Hi! How are you?*
Puppet B: *I'm fine. How are you?*
Puppet A: *I'm fine, thank you.*

b. Pupils repeat each line of dialogue three times, in chorus.

4. Practise.
a. Divide class into two groups and say dialogue twice so that each group practises both parts.
b. Practise dialogue using **Conversation Lines** (see page 6).

OPEN YOUR BOOKS

Open your Pupil's Book to page 14. Show it to pupils and ask them to name the characters. T: *What's her name?* (Option: Pupils say, in own language, what they think picture is about.)

1. Pupils open their books to page 14.
a. Play cassette. Pupils listen and point to character who is speaking.

Lisa: *Hi, Andy. How are you?*
Andy: *I'm fine. How are you?*
Lisa: *I'm fine, thank you.*

b. Play cassette again, stopping after each line. Pupils repeat line.

2. Present sample structures and contraction.
a. Write sample structures on board. Read them aloud, pointing to words. Pupils repeat.
b. Write explanation of contraction on board: *I am = I'm.*
c. Pupils practise *I am fine* and *I'm fine.* Point to explanation on board as you practise.

3. Practise.
In pairs, pupils practise dialogue with contracted form *I'm,* using own names. Teacher should circulate, helping as necessary.

EXTENSION

1. Beanbag Game (see page 6). Pupils stand in a circle (or remain seated). P1 tosses beanbag or ball to P2.

P1: *Hi, (Paul). How are you?*
P2: *I'm fine, thank you.*

Then P2 tosses beanbag/ball to another pupil. **NOTE:** If pupils can't remember each other's names at this stage, they can ask *What's your name?* before greeting.

WORKBOOK page 17

- Pupils name characters and trace two sentences. Then they practise question and answer pattern.
- Pupils trace answer. Then they practise question and answer pattern.

Let's Sing

LANGUAGE PATTERNS: Hi! How are you? I'm fine, thank you.

VOCABULARY: General review

MATERIALS: tape-recorder and cassette; two puppets or soft toys; two paper cups and string

REVIEW

1. Divide class into two groups and practise greetings. Group A: *Hi! How are you?* Group B: *I'm fine, thank you.* Reverse roles.

2. Sing 'The Hello Song'.
a. Pupils sing with cassette.
b. Pupils sing again, using own names in song. Pupils can role-play as they sing.

PRESENTATION

1. Review dialogue.
a. Use puppets to model question and answer.

Puppet A: *Hi! How are you?*
Puppet B: *I'm fine, thank you.*

b. Pupils repeat each line of dialogue three times, in chorus.

2. Practise.
Divide class into two groups. Do a competitive **Chain Drill** to practise question and answer. The object is to see which group can be first to correctly complete drill (see page 6).

OPEN YOUR BOOKS

Open your Pupil's Book to page 15. Show it to pupils and ask them to name the characters.

1. Pupils open their books to page 15.

a. Play cassette.
Hi, how are you?
I'm fine.
Hi, how are you?
I'm fine.
Hi, how are you?
I'm fine. How are you?
I'm fine, I'm fine, I'm fine.

Hi, how are you?
I'm fine. How are you?
Hi, how are you?
I'm fine.
Hi, how are you?
I'm fine. How are you?
I'm fine, I'm fine, I'm fine.

b. Play cassette again. Pupils sing along.

2. Practise.
Sing song in two groups.

Group A: *Hi, how are you?*
Group B: *I'm fine.*
etc.

EXTENSION

1. Play Telephone Call. Divide class into pairs and give each pair a 'telephone'. (Use two paper cups and a long string. Make a hole in bottom of each cup. Insert string into each hole and knot it at each end.)

P1: *Hi! How are you?*
P2: *I'm fine. How are you?*
P1: *I'm fine, thank you.*

Let's Learn

LANGUAGE PATTERNS: What colour is this? It's (red).

NEW VOCABULARY: Colours: red, blue, green, yellow, orange, pink, purple, brown, black, grey, white

MATERIALS: classroom objects or magazine pictures for Unit 1 vocabulary; large squares of paper in colours listed above; two puppets or soft toys; tape-recorder and cassette

REVIEW

1. Quickly show realia/pictures to review Unit 1 vocabulary.

T: *What's this?*
Ps: *It's (a pen).*

2. In pairs, pupils practise question and answer pattern using realia. Teacher should circulate, helping as necessary.

PRESENTATION

1. Present new vocabulary.
a. Show pupils red-coloured square and name colour. Pupils repeat three times.

T: *Red. Red.*
Ps: *Red.*

b. Point to three red objects in classroom, saying *Red.* Pupils repeat.
c. Pupils find other red objects in classroom. They point to each object and say *Red.*
d. Repeat Steps **a–c** for remaining colours.

2. Present pattern.
a. Use puppets and coloured squares to model question and answer.

Puppet A: *What colour is this?* (Holding or pointing to coloured square.)
Puppet B: *It's (red).*

b. Pupils repeat each line of dialogue three times, in chorus.
c. Continue with other colours.

3. Practise.
a. Divide class into two groups. Use coloured squares and coloured objects to cue groups.

Group A: *What colour is this?*
Group B: *It's (red).*

Reverse roles. Repeat for all colours.
b. In pairs, pupils ask each other about colours of their belongings or clothing. Teacher should circulate, checking.

OPEN YOUR BOOKS

Open your Pupil's Book to page 16. Show it to pupils and ask them to name the characters. (Option: Pupils say, in own language, what they think picture is about.)

1. Pupils open their books to page 16.
a. Play cassette (dialogue only). Pupils listen and point to character who is speaking.

Lisa: *What colour is this?*
Jenny: *It's red.*

b. Play cassette again, stopping after each line. Pupils repeat line.

2. Present sample structures and contraction.
a. Write structures on board. Read them aloud, pointing to words. Pupils repeat.
b. Write explanation of contraction on board: *It is = It's.*
c. Pupils practise *It is red* and *It's red.* Point to explanation on board as you practise.

3. Practise.
Divide class into two groups. Practise question and answer pattern with the colour pictures on PB page 17, using cats as models. One group is the Black Cat and the other is the Orange Cat. Then reverse roles.

4. 'The Black Cat Song.'
a. Ask pupils to look at the picture at bottom of page 17 and name the colours.
b. Play song on cassette. Pupils listen and point to each object.

Green grass, (echo)
Blue skies, (echo)
Black cats, (echo)
Yellow eyes. (chorus)

Red birds, (echo)
Blue skies, (echo)
Black cats, yellow eyes. (chorus)

White clouds, (echo)
Blue skies, (echo)
Black cats, yellow eyes. (chorus)

Black cats, (echo)
Blue skies, (echo)
Yellow, yellow eyes. (chorus)

c. Play cassette again. Pupils sing along.
d. Sing song in two groups. One group sings the phrase first and the other group repeats it. All pupils sing chorus lines.

(Continued on page 22.)

EXTENSION

1. Ask several pupils to look silently round classroom for a red object. When called on, pupil names colour and object.

T: *Red.*
P1: *A red pen.* (Pointing to pen.)
T: *Yes. A red pen.*

Repeat for all colours.

2. The Right Choice (see page 7). Divide class into two teams. Place coloured squares on board rail. One pupil from each team, in turn, comes up and stands by board. Teacher names a colour (*blue*). Pupil chooses correct square and wins a point for team.

WORKBOOK pages 18 and 19

page 18

- Pupils trace names of colours on labels. Then they colour each jar to match name.
- Pupils complete sentence at bottom of page with name of colour on adjoining jar. (**Answer:** *blue.*)

page 19

- Pupils colour seven objects at top of page, using colours of their choice. They trace colour name *black*. Then write names of other colours under objects.
- Pupils trace dotted letters. Then they complete colour names by writing letters in blanks. (**Answers:** *purple, orange, yellow, grey, brown, white.*)

Let's Learn Some More

LANGUAGE PATTERNS: What colour is it? It's (blue). This is a (blue) book. This is a (red) and (yellow) (book).

VOCABULARY: Review colours and classroom objects

MATERIALS: classroom objects or magazine pictures (if possible slightly different from those used in Let's Learn) for Unit 1 vocabulary; tape-recorder and cassette; 6 red and 6 blue paper squares; multi-coloured classroom objects

REVIEW

1. Divide class into two groups. Use realia/pictures for Unit 1 vocabulary to cue groups. Show an object to each group in turn. Teacher holds up (bag).

T: *What's this?*
Group A: *It's (a bag).*

2. Review 'The Black Cat Song'.
a. Ask pupils to look at picture at bottom of PB page 17 and name the colours.
b. Sing song with cassette.

PRESENTATION

1. Present question and answer pattern.
a. Show (a book) to pupils as you model questions and answers.

T: *What's this?*
Ps: *It's (a book).*
T: *What colour is it?*
Ps: *It's (blue).*
T: *(Yes). This is a (blue) (book).*

b. Practise the other colours with various objects.

2. Practise.
a. Divide class into two groups to practise question and answer patterns. Use realia/pictures for Unit 1 vocabulary to cue pupils. One pupil holds an object for group. Pupils ask and answer questions as a group.

Group A: *What's this?*
Group B: *It's (a bag).*
Group A: *What colour is it?*
Group B: *It's (red).*
Group A: *(Yes). This is a (red) (bag).*

b. In pairs, pupils continue to practise pattern, using classroom objects. Teacher should circulate, helping as necessary.

3. Present second part of pattern.
a. Hold up a book and name colours on cover.

T: *This is a (red) and (yellow) (book).*

b. Pupils repeat three times, in chorus.

4. Practise.
Select a pupil volunteer. Give pupil a classroom object with two colours on it. Pupil describes object to class. Class repeats description. Repeat with several pupils.

OPEN YOUR BOOKS

Open your Pupil's Book to page 18. Show it to pupils and ask them to name the characters. (Option: Pupils say, in own language, what they think each picture is about.)

1. Pupils open their books to page 18.
a. Play cassette. Pupils listen and point to objects.

Teacher: *What's this?*
All: *It's a book.*
Teacher: *What colour is it?*
All: *It's blue.*
Teacher: *This is a blue book.*
Kate: *This is a red and yellow book.*

b. Play cassette again, stopping after each line. Pupils repeat line.

2. Present sample structures.
a. Write structures on board. Read them aloud, pointing to words. Pupils repeat.
b. Hold up various classroom objects and describe them with pupils.

T and Ps: *This is an (orange) (pencil). This is a (blue) and (orange) (book).*

3. Practise.
Look at activity at top of PB page 19.
a. Model the language pattern presented by cats. Pupils repeat.
b. Divide class into two groups. Groups take turns making statements about pictures as they point to them in order.

Group A: *This is a (red) and (blue) (bag).*
Group B: *This is a (purple) (pencil).*

c. In pairs, pupils continue practice, using same picture cues. Each pupil should make a statement about all pictures. Teacher should circulate, helping as necessary.

EXTENSION

1. Memory Chain (see page 7). Divide class into two or three teams. In turn, each team tries to make chain as long as possible, without forgetting any items. Each pupil in team adds one item to list.

P1: *This is (a red book).*
P2: *This is (a red book) and this is (a yellow pencil).*

2. Guessing Game (see page 6). A pupil volunteer thinks of an object in the classroom and describes colours. Class guesses what object is.

P1: *It's (blue) and (red) and (black).*
Ps: *It's (a book).*
P1: *Yes./No.*

Continue with other volunteers.

(Continued on page 24.)

WORKBOOK pages 20 and 21

page 20

- Pupils colour classroom objects to match colour names. Then they trace words and read sentences aloud.

page 21

- Pupils colour desk and pencil at top of page in colours of their choice. Then they trace words. Then they write a question and answer for desk and pencil. (**Answers:** Each question will be *What colour is it?* Answers will depend on colours chosen.)
- Pupils read sentences aloud. Then they colour each object as indicated.

A	B	C
a	b	c

Let's Learn the Alphabet

NEW VOCABULARY: apple, cat

MATERIALS: tape-recorder and cassette; lined paper

1. Review alphabet by singing 'The Alphabet Song'.

2. Pupils open their books to bottom of page 19.

a. Play cassette. Pupils listen and point to letters.

Teacher: *A, apple; B, book; C, cat.*

b. Play cassette again, stopping after each letter. Pupils repeat letter and word.

c. Say word *apple* carefully, emphasizing initial sound. Print word *apple* on board and underline *a*.

d. Print letter *a* next to word *apple* on board.

a—apple

Ask pupils to think of other words that begin with the same sound (e.g. *and*).

e. Repeat Steps **c** and **d** for words *book* and *cat*.

3. Show pupils how to print a small *a*. Then introduce capital *A*. Repeat for letters *B* and *C*. Practise printing letters on lined paper.

WORKBOOK page 22

- Pupils draw a line from each object to the letter it begins with. Then they trace names of objects.
- Pupils circle letter each object begins with.
- Pupils trace first letter of each word.

Let's Move

LANGUAGE PATTERNS: put your hand up, put your hand down, take out your book, put your book away, pick up your pencil, put your pencil down, write your name, look at the board

NEW VOCABULARY: hand, board

MATERIALS: tape-recorder and cassette

REVIEW

1. Review colours and sing 'The Black Cat Song' with cassette.

2. Ask pupil volunteers to give commands from Unit 1 to class. Cue them by pointing to pictures on PB page 12, if necessary.

PRESENTATION

1. Present commands.
a. Model command phrases using clear gestures.
b. Say commands. Pupils listen and do commands.
c. Repeat commands. Pupils listen, repeat, and do commands.
d. Divide class into two groups. Give a pair of commands to one group at a time. Each group does and says commands. Alternate between groups. Practise all commands, varying pace. Then one group gives the other group commands to do.

2. Play a game.
Divide class into teams. Give a pair of commands to one pupil on each team. Award a point if actions are done correctly.

OPEN YOUR BOOKS

Open your Pupil's Book to page 20 and show it to pupils. Say command for each picture. Pupils repeat and do command.

1. Pupils open their books to page 20.
a. Play cassette. Pupils listen and point to each action.

Put your hand up.
Put your hand down.
Take out your book.
Put your book away.
Pick up your pencil.
Put your pencil down.
Write your name.
Look at the board.

b. Play cassette again, stopping after each command. Pupils repeat command.

2. Call out commands in random order. Pupils repeat and do commands.

3. Each pupil, in turn, points to a picture and gives command (with teacher's help). Class repeats and does command.

EXTENSION

1. Divide class into two teams. Act out a command for each team in turn. Award a point if team guesses command correctly.

WORKBOOK page 23

- Pupils draw a line from each picture to matching command. Then they say command.

Let's Listen

LANGUAGE PATTERNS: Unit review

VOCABULARY: Unit review

MATERIALS: classroom objects of various colours; box; tape-recorder and cassette; ball or beanbag

REVIEW

1. Let's Talk.

a. Conversation Lines (see page 6). Pupils say *How are you?* dialogue from Let's Talk.

b. Divide class into two teams. One pupil from each team comes to front of class. The two pupils greet each other. Award a point to team if greeting is correct.

2. Let's Learn.

a. Classify objects by colour. Gather classroom objects of different colours (several different objects of each colour). Hold up each object in turn.

T: *What colour is this?*
Ps: *It's (yellow).*

b. Colour interview. In pairs, pupils ask each other about the colour of their belongings or pieces of clothing. Teacher should circulate, checking. Limit activity to one or two minutes.

3. Let's Learn Some More.
Place a variety of colourful classroom objects in box. One pupil comes up to front, chooses an object, and identifies it.

P1: *This is (a pencil).*
Ps: *What colour is it?*
P1: *It's (red).*
Ps: *This is a (red) (pencil).*
Repeat with other pupils.

4. Let's Move.

a. Quickly review commands from Let's Move. Then do a **Command Chain** exercise (see page 5). Whole class must listen to all the commands and do the actions *after* you complete chain.

b. Ask pupil volunteers to give commands to whole class.

PRESENTATION

Teach pupils how to do test. Put two classroom objects on board rail. Ask one pupil to stand next to board. Make a statement about the colour of one of the objects. T: *It's (purple).* Pupil chooses correct object and teacher ticks board above object.

NOTE: If you want to conduct this as a formal test, go immediately to Step **1b** in Open Your Books.

OPEN YOUR BOOKS

1. Pupils open their books to page 21.

a. Play cassette. Pupils point to correct picture.

1. *It's purple.*
2. *It's pink.*
3. *What colour is this?*
   It's green.
4. *What colour is this?*
   It's orange.
5. *This is a yellow ruler.*
6. *This is a blue and white desk.*
7. *Put your hand up.*
8. *Put your book away.*

b. Play cassette again. Each pupil does exercise as a written test.

2. Correct test with pupils.

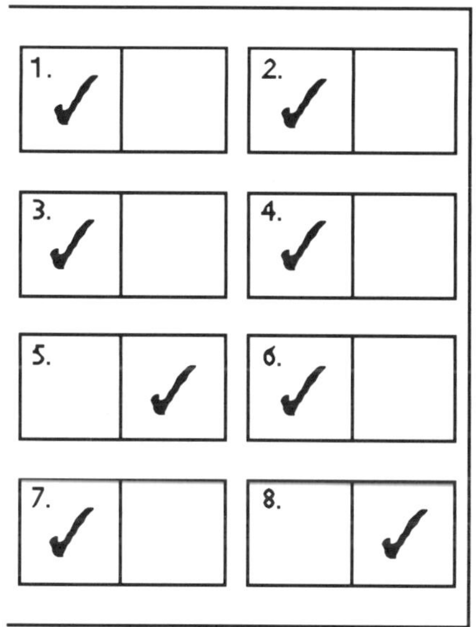

EXTENSION

1. Charades (see page 6). Several pupils, in turn, act out commands from Let's Move, using PB page 20 to help them if necessary. Class guesses command.

2. Beanbag Game (see page 6). Pupils form a circle. Give ball or beanbag to one pupil. P1 tosses ball to P2, points to P2's (shirt) and asks *What colour is this?* P2 answers, and tosses ball to P3. Continue until all pupils have answered a question about the colour of their clothing.

WORKBOOK page 24

- Pupils colour jars to match colour names. Then they trace dotted words. Then they complete each phrase with a colour name of their choice. Then they draw a line from paintbrush above each object to matching colour name.
- Pupils trace letters of the alphabet.

Let's Review

LANGUAGE PATTERNS: General review

VOCABULARY: General review

MATERIALS: classroom objects or magazine pictures for Unit 1 vocabulary; tape-recorder and cassette; small multi-coloured objects or pictures of objects for Unit 1 vocabulary, different from those above; bags; sets of dice

REVIEW

1. Songs.
Whole class sings 'The Hello Song' and 'Hi! How Are You?' Role-play greetings from songs, using waving actions and handshakes. Use front of class as stage and ask pupils, in groups of 3–4, to act out meeting each other for first time.

2. Vocabulary.
Put a collection of realia/pictures for Unit 1 vocabulary on large desk or table at the front of classroom. There should be more than one of each item, and total number of items should equal number of pupils. All pupils should stand.

a. Teacher says name of an object. T: *(Ruler)*. First pupil goes up to front, takes (ruler) and returns to seat. Teacher then says another object. T: *(Pencil)*. Continue until all objects have been claimed. Every pupil should now be sitting down and holding an object.
b. Teacher says name of object. T: *(Pen)*. All pupils holding pens go up to front, put them on the desk or table, and then return to their seats. Continue until all objects have been replaced.

3. Structures.
Place small multi-coloured objects/pictures for Unit 1 vocabulary in a bag. Pass bag around class. Each pupil, in turn, pulls object from bag and names it. P1: *This is a (blue) and (purple) (ruler).*

4. Commands.
Use multi-coloured objects and pupils' own objects to practise commands from Units 1 and 2. Ask pupils, one at a time, to perform the actions you give them. Combine verbs with various nouns and colours from Units 1 and 2. Some examples are: *Open your bag. Take out your eraser. Put your eraser away. Stand up. Touch the orange chair. Look at the orange and brown desk. Point to the purple pen. Sit down.*

OPEN YOUR BOOKS

1. Say these.
Pupils open their books to page 22. Teacher circulates, checking, as pupils do the following activities.

a. Pupils review vocabulary by pointing to each picture in order, calling out name of picture, in chorus. (**Answers:** *a book, a bag, a pencil, a desk, a chair, a ruler, a pen, an eraser, a teacher, a cat.*)
b. Divide class into pairs. Give each pair a dice. Pupils take turns rolling dice, moving number of spaces equal to number on dice, and identifying picture. Pupils continue until one pupil lands directly on goal.
c. Divide class into pairs. P1 identifies all picture cues as quickly as possible. P2 listens and helps P1 if necessary. If all pictures are identified correctly, P1 receives 10 points. Reverse roles and play again.

2. Play a game.
Pupils form groups of 3–4 to play Colour Game at bottom of page 22. One pupil from each group places the middle of a pencil in the centre of the colour wheel and spins it. Then all pupils name the colour under the point of the pencil. P1 asks *What colour is this?* Group answers *It's (red).* Continue so that all pupils spin pencil and ask question. Teacher circulates, checking.

3. Say and act.
a. Look at pictures at top of PB page 23. Point to answer speech bubble in first picture and say *My name is John.* Point to speech bubble with question mark and ask pupils to guess what should be there. (**Answer**: *What's your name?*) Repeat for second picture. (**Answer**: *I'm fine, thank you.*)
b. In pairs, pupils practise both dialogues. Teacher should circulate, helping as necessary.

4. Ask your partner.
a. Review *What's this?* Model the pattern for the class and point to an object.

T: *What's this?*
Ps: *It's a desk.*

Pupils continue exercise in pairs, using page 23 in Pupil's Book. Teacher should circulate, helping as necessary.
b. Review *Is this a (blue) (desk)?* Hold up Teacher's Book and point to brown desk.

T: *Is this a blue desk?*
Ps: *No, it isn't. It's a brown desk.*

5. Listen carefully.
a. Play cassette. Pupils listen and point to correct picture.

a: *Put your ruler away.*
b: *Pick up your eraser.*

b. Play cassette again. Pupils listen and tick small box next to correct answer.

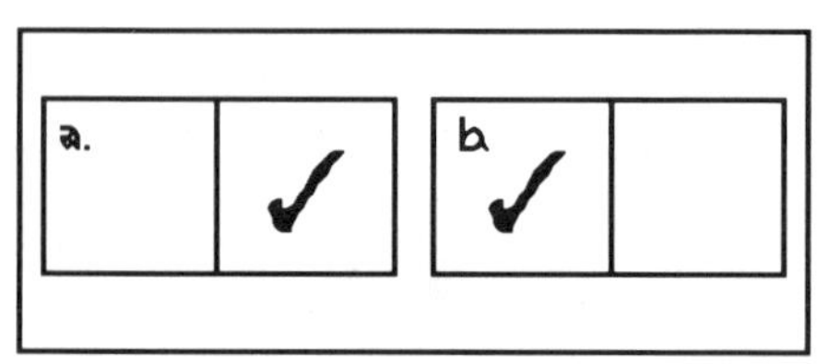

(Continued on page 29.)

c. Pupils identify other two pictures and say commands. (*Take your ruler out. Put your eraser down.*) Then they say all four commands.

EXTENSION

1. Treasure Hunt (see page 7). Give pupils a verbal list of objects to 'find' in classroom (a blue book, a red pencil, etc.). Keep list short enough to be remembered (three or four objects). Pupils must 'hunt' for these objects by looking round classroom while remaining seated. When they have found all objects, they put their hands up. When all pupils are ready ask a pupil volunteer to point to or stand by object.

P1: *What's this?*
Ps: *It's a (red) (pencil).*

Continue with other objects.

WORKBOOK pages 25 and 26

page 25
- Pupils trace capital and small letters in grid.

page 26
- Pupils write first letter of each word in blank. Then they draw a line from each letter to object and then to name of object.
- Pupils circle correct name for each object. Then they complete sentences below. (**Answers:** *It is a book. It is a ruler.*) Then they practise question and answer pattern.
- Pupils write appropriate colour name in blank in each sentence. Then they colour jars and objects.

Unit Three

Let's Talk

LANGUAGE PATTERNS: Hi, (John). This is my friend, (Sarah). Hello, (Kate). Let's play.

NEW VOCABULARY: Let's, play, friend

MATERIALS: squares of coloured paper (as for Unit 2); three puppets or soft toys; tape-recorder and cassette

REVIEW

1. Find Your Partners (see page 6). Give each pupil a piece of coloured paper. There should be several slips of each colour. Teacher holds up one piece of coloured paper and says (*Red*). Pupils holding red slips stand and greet each other, in turn, using own names. Continue with other colours.

P1: *Hello, (Kate). How are you?*
P2: *I'm fine, thank you.*

2. Practise commands from Units 1 and 2 in quick succession, first with whole class, and then with individual pupils.

PRESENTATION

1. Present pattern.
a. Use three puppets to model dialogue. Ask a pupil to hold Puppet C.

NOTE: Puppets should point to each other as they do introductions. If your classroom puppets have names, use these where indicated.

Puppet A: *Hi, (John). This is my friend, (Sarah).* (Indicating Puppet C.)
Puppet B: *Hello, (Sarah).*
(To Puppet C.)
Puppet C: *Hi, (John).*
All: *Let's play!*

b. Pupils repeat each part of dialogue three times, in chorus. Give special attention to *This is my friend, (Sarah).*

2. Practise.
Divide class into three groups to practise dialogue. Each group says one part. Repeat three times so that each group says each part.

OPEN YOUR BOOKS

Open your Pupil's Book to page 24. Show it to pupils and ask them to name the characters. (Option: Pupils say, in own language, what they think picture is about.)

1. Pupils open their books to page 24.
a. Play cassette. Pupils listen and point to character who is speaking.

Kate: *Hi, John. This is my friend, Sarah.*
John: *Hello, Sarah.*
Sarah: *Hi, John.*
All: *Let's play.*

b. Play cassette again, stopping after each line. Pupils repeat line.

2. Present sample structure.
Write structure on board. Read it aloud, pointing to words. Pupils repeat.

NOTE: Let's is always used in contracted form.

3. Practise.
Divide class into three groups, each group representing one character. Pupils repeat dialogue without cassette.

EXTENSION

1. Divide class into groups of three. Pupils practise dialogue, using own names.

WORKBOOK page 27

- Pupils name characters and draw a line from each balloon to correct child's hand. Then they trace words in bubbles.
- Pupils trace beginning of sentence. Then they complete it with name of a friend. Then they draw picture of friend.

Let's Sing

LANGUAGE PATTERNS: Hi, (Kate). This is my friend, (Sarah). Hello, (John). Let's play.

VOCABULARY: Unit review

MATERIALS: two puppets or soft toys; tape-recorder and cassette

REVIEW

1. Sing 'Hi, How Are You?'

2. Practise commands from Units 1 and 2.

a. Give a series of commands. Pupils do commands.
b. Ask pupil volunteers to give commands for class to do. Use pictures on pages 12 and 20 of Pupil's Book to prompt volunteers if necessary.

PRESENTATION

1. Review dialogue from Let's Talk. Use puppets to model dialogue.

Puppet A: *This is my friend, (Sarah).*
Class: *Hello, (Sarah).*
Puppet B: *This is my friend, (John).*
Class: *Hi, (John).*
All: *Let's play.*

Puppets point to each other as they do introductions.

2. Practise.
Ask two pupils to go to front of class and introduce each other to class.
P1: *This is my friend, (Sarah).*
Whole class will greet each pupil with *Hi* or *Hello* after the introduction.

OPEN YOUR BOOKS

Open your Pupil's Book to page 25. Show it to pupils and ask them to name the two main characters, John and Sarah. (Option: Pupils say, in own language, what they think picture is about.)

1. Pupils open their books to page 25.
a. Play cassette. Pupils listen and point to character who is speaking.

This is my friend, Sarah.
Hello, Sarah.
This is my friend, Sarah.
Hello, Sarah.

This is my friend, John.
Hi, John!
This is my friend, John.
Hi, John!

This is my friend, Sarah.
This is my friend, John.
Let's play!

b. Play cassette again. Pupils sing along.

2. Practise.
Divide class into two groups, each group representing a character. Sing the song, then reverse roles and sing it again.

EXTENSION

1. Divide pupils into groups of three and practise introductions, one group at a time. P1 introduces P2 to P3. Then all three say *Let's play*. Change roles so every pupil has a chance to introduce a friend.

Let's Learn

LANGUAGE PATTERNS: What's this? It's (a pencil case). What are these? They're (cassettes).

NEW VOCABULARY: a cassette, a pencil case, a crayon, a table, a marker, a notebook (singular and plural forms)

MATERIALS: classroom objects or magazine pictures for Unit 1 vocabulary; classroom objects (as listed above); puppets or soft toys; tape-recorder and cassette; pupils' bags

REVIEW

1. Review vocabulary and question and answer pattern from Unit 1. Place realia/pictures for Unit 1 vocabulary on board rail. Point to each and ask:

T: *What's this?*
Ps: *It's (a pencil).*

2. Divide class into two groups to review colours. Point to object/picture on rail. Group A names object and asks Group B to name colour.

Group A: *This is (a ruler). What colour is it?*
Group B: *It's (pink).*

PRESENTATION

1. Present new vocabulary.
a. Use realia to introduce new vocabulary. Introduce new words one at a time. Pupils repeat each word several times. After introducing each new word, conduct a quick mini-drill, alternating new word with previously introduced words.

T: *A pencil case, a pencil case.*
Ps: *A pencil case.*

b. Quickly pass objects round class to practise new vocabulary. Pupil says name of each object as he or she passes it.

2. Review *What's this? It's a (crayon).* while practising new vocabulary.
a. Put realia for new vocabulary on table at front of class. Ask two volunteers to come up. Give each an object, in turn. One at a time, volunteers show objects to class.

P1: *What's this?*
Ps: *It's (a crayon).*

b. Do a modified **Chain Drill** (see page 6). If rows are of equal length, use those. If not, divide class into two teams. Give an object to first pupil in each row/team. P1 turns to P2 directly behind, and shows object.

P1: *What's this?*
P2: *It's (a crayon). What's this?* (to P3), etc.

When object reaches last pupil in each row or team, pupil holds object up. The first row/team to finish wins a point. Redistribute objects and play again, starting with last pupil in row/team.

3. Present pattern.
a. Use puppets to model plural question and answer. Hold up two cassettes and then put them on table/board rail.

Puppet A: *What are these?*
Puppet B: *They're cassettes.*

(Emphasize the *s* sound at the end of the plural words.)
b. Pupils repeat each line of dialogue three times, in chorus.

4. Practise.
Draw pictures of new vocabulary items on board. For each object draw one item and also a small group of items (number does not matter). Point to drawing of several (cassettes) and ask pupils to name objects.

T: *What are these?*
Ps: *They're (cassettes).*

Then point to drawing of a (table).

T: *What is this?*
Ps: *It's a (table).*

Continue practice with singular and plural forms of all words. Pupil volunteers can ask some of the questions. After the whole class has practised several times, pupils could continue practice in pairs.

OPEN YOUR BOOKS

Open your Pupil's Book to page 26. Show it to pupils and ask them to name the characters. (Option: Pupils say, in own language, what they think picture is about.)

1. Pupils open their books to page 26.
a. Play cassette. Pupils listen and point to character who is speaking.

Jenny: *What's this?*
Scott: *It's a pencil case.*
Andy: *What are these?*
Kate: *They're cassettes.*

b. Play cassette again, stopping after each line. Pupils repeat line.

2. Present sample structures and contraction.
a. Write structures on board. Read them aloud, pointing to words. Pupils repeat.
b. Write explanation of contraction on board: *They are = They're.*
c. Pupils practise *They are cassettes* and *They're cassettes.* Point to explanation on board as you practise.

(Continued on page 33.)

3. Practise.

a. Divide class into two groups. Practise question and answer patterns with new vocabulary on PB page 27, using cats as models.

b. In pairs, pupils continue question and answer practice.

4. Look at activity at bottom of page 27. Pupils point to pictures and make sentences following model.

a. Do this as a whole class.

b. Continue in pairs.

EXTENSION

1. Show and Tell. Pupils name objects in their bags.

a. One pupil brings bag to front of class. Pupil takes out object and asks class to name it in a complete sentence. Pupils must use *This is a* _______ and *These are* _______ in their sentences.

b. Continue practice in pairs.

2. Practise singular and plural forms of vocabulary from Unit 1. Use realia/ pictures. Give one object/picture to each pupil. Pupils show objects, one at a time, and ask class to name them, asking *What's this?* or *What are these?*

WORKBOOK pages 28 and 29

page 28

- Pupils trace sample questions and answers. Then they write question and answer for each picture, using contractions. (**Answers**: *What's this? It's a crayon. / What's this? It's a notebook. / What are these? They're chairs. / What's this? It's a desk.)*
- Pupils draw lines from full forms to matching contractions. (**Answers:** *They are—They're / What is — What's / I am — I'm / It is not — It isn't.)*

page 29

- Pupils circle correct label (singular or plural) next to each picture.
- Pupils circle correct sentence next to each picture. (**Answers**: *These are markers. These are tables. This is a cassette.*) Then they trace words.

Let's Learn Some More

LANGUAGE PATTERNS: How many (trainers)? Ten (trainers).

NEW VOCABULARY: trainers(s), numbers one – ten

MATERIALS: multiple classroom objects for Units 1 and 3 vocabulary (cassettes, pencils, crayons, notebooks, pens, rulers); pair of trainers; tape-recorder and cassette

REVIEW

1. Sing 'This is My Friend'.

2. Question and answer review. Divide class into two groups. Hold up one classroom object or several of the same kind. Group A asks question and Group B answers. Then reverse roles.

Group A: *What's this?*
Group B: *It's (a crayon).*
Group A: *What are these?*
Group B: *They're (cassettes).*

PRESENTATION

1. Present new vocabulary.
a. Write numbers *1–10* on board. Below each number, write word. Count from 1 to 10, pointing to each word.
b. Pupils count from *one* to *ten* with you as you place ten markers or crayons, one at a time, on desk in front of you.

2. Present pattern.
a. Show one pencil to pupils. Ask question *How many pencils?* and give answer *One*. Then show pupils four pencils.

T: *How many pencils? One, two, three, four…four pencils.*
How many pencils?
Ps: *Four pencils.*

b. Put five books on board rail and repeat pattern.

T: *How many books?*
Ps: *One, two, three, four, five…five books.*

Repeat pattern several times, using other classroom objects.

OPEN YOUR BOOKS

Open your Pupil's Book to page 28 and show it to pupils. They count purple trainers as you point to each in turn.

1. Pupils open their books to page 28.
a. Play cassette. Pupils listen and point to numbered trainers.

One little, two little, three little trainers,
Four little, five little, six little trainers,
Seven little, eight little, nine little trainers
Ten little purple trainers.

How many trainers?
Ten trainers!

Ten little, nine little, eight little trainers,
Seven little, six little, five little trainers,
Four little, three little, two little trainers,
One little purple trainer.

How many trainers?
One trainer!

b. Play cassette again. Pupils sing along.
c. Look at activity at bottom of PB page 28. T: *How many trainers?* Pupils count and answer.

2. Practise.
Look at the activity at top of page 29.
a. Model question and answer presented by cats. Pupils repeat.
b. Divide class into two groups. Pupils point to pictures in order. In turn, each group asks the other a question about a picture.
c. In pairs, pupils continue practice, using picture cues in book.

EXTENSION

1. Select group of ten pupils. One pupil stands up and class says *One pupil.* The next pupil stands up and class says *Two pupils,* etc.

WORKBOOK pages 30 and 31

page 30
- Pupils trace numbers. Then they draw a line from each number to group with same number of objects. Then they write number on line next to each group.
- Pupils trace words.

page 31
- Pupils draw lines from sentences on left to appropriate responses on right. (**Answers**: *Is this a pen? No, it isn't. It's a pencil. / What's this? It's a bag. / What colour is it? It's blue and red. / Hi, Jenny. How are you? I'm fine, thank you. / Hello, Lisa. Hello, Kate. / What are these? They're markers.*)
- Pupils trace sample label. Then they write label for each group of objects on line next to picture. (**Answers**: *ten markers, five cassettes, eight pencils, four cats, three pencil cases.*)

Let's Learn the Alphabet

NEW VOCABULARY: egg, fish

MATERIALS: tape-recorder and cassette; lined paper

1. Review A-B-C letter sequence.
T: *A–apple, B–book, C–cat.*

2. Pupils open their books to bottom of page 29.

a. Play cassette. Pupils listen and point to letters.

Teacher: *D, desk; E, egg; F, fish.*

b. Play cassette again, stopping after each letter. Pupils repeat letter and word.
c. Say word *desk* carefully, emphasizing initial sound. Print word *desk* on board and underline *d.*
d. Print letter *d* next to word *desk* on board.

d—desk

Ask pupils to think of other words that begin with the same sound (e.g. *door*).
e. Repeat Steps **c** and **d** for words *egg* and *fish.* (Other words are, e.g.: *eraser, friend.*)

3. Show pupils how to print a small *d.* Then introduce capital *D.* Repeat for letters *E* and *F.* Practise printing letters on lined paper.

WORKBOOK page 32

- Pupils draw a line from each object to its initial letter, then to matching object, then to name. Then they trace names.
- Pupils trace letters.

Let's Move

LANGUAGE PATTERNS: make a circle/two lines, go to the door, come here, count the girls/boys, draw a picture, give me the crayon

NEW VOCABULARY: circle, lines, door, girls, boys, picture

MATERIALS: tape-recorder and cassette

REVIEW

1. Sing 'The Purple Trainer Song' to review numbers. Assign each pupil a number from 1 to 10. Pupils stand as their numbers are sung.

2. Quickly review all commands from Units 1 and 2. Say chains of commands for pupils to act out.

PRESENTATION

1. Present commands.
a. Model command phrases using clear gestures. For *Make a circle* and *Make two lines,* move a small group of pupils to demonstrate.
b. Say commands. Pupils listen and do commands.
c. Repeat commands. Pupils listen, repeat, and do commands.
d. Divide class into two groups. Give a command to one group at a time. Group repeats and does command. Practise all commands, varying speed. Then a few individual pupils from one group could, in turn, give other group commands to do.

2. Play a game.
Divide class into teams. Give a command to one pupil on each team. If action is done correctly, award a team point.

OPEN YOUR BOOKS

Open your Pupil's Book to page 30 and show it to pupils. Point to each picture in turn and say command. Pupils repeat command.

1. Pupils open their books to page 30.
a. Play cassette. Pupils listen and point to each action.

Make a circle.
Make two lines.
Go to the door.
Come here.
Count the girls.
Count the boys.
Draw a picture.
Give me the crayon.

b. Play cassette again, stopping after each command. Pupils say command.

2. Say commands in random order. Pupils point to correct pictures and repeat commands.

3. Use pupil volunteers to do commands given by other pupils. Each pupil, in turn, points to a picture and gives command (with teacher's help). Class repeats command. Volunteer performs actions.

EXTENSION

1. Charades (see page 6). Several pupils, in turn, act out commands, using PB page 30 to help them if necessary. Class must guess command.

2. Divide class into two teams. Call out a command and point to a pupil in Team A. Pupil does command. Then give a command to Team B. Continue with all commands. Award a point if action is done correctly.

3. Review all commands from Units 1–3. Then practise variations of commands. Example: *Count the (pencils). Go to (the board).*

WORKBOOK page 33

- Pupils draw a line from each command to matching picture. Then they say command.
- Pupils circle correct word for number of people in each picture. (**Answers**: *two, five.*) Then they write number, in letters, on grid. Then they trace words.

Let's Listen

LANGUAGE PATTERNS: Unit review

VOCABULARY: Unit review

MATERIALS: multiple classroom objects for Let's Learn vocabulary (two or three crayons, pencil cases, cassettes, markers, notebooks); tape-recorder and cassette

REVIEW

1. Let's Talk.

a. Divide pupils into pairs. Point to a pupil and ask each pair, in turn, to introduce each other to that pupil.

P1: *Hi, (John). This is my friend, (Kate).*
P2: *Hello, (Kate).*
P3: *Hi, (John).*

2. Let's Learn.

a. Put classroom objects for Let's Learn vocabulary on table in front of class. Hold up one object or several of same kind. Pupils describe object(s). Ps: *It's (a cassette)./They are (cassettes).*

b. Divide class into two groups. Hold up object(s). Group A asks *What is it?* or *What are they?* Group B answers *It's (a cassette)* or *They're (cassettes).* Reverse roles and continue with other objects.

3. Let's Learn Some More

a. Put multiple classroom objects on table. Divide class into two teams. Point to objects. T: *How many (cassettes)?* P1 from Team A goes to table, counts objects, and calls out answer. P1: *(One, two). (Two) (cassettes).* Continue with a pupil from Team B. Award a point for each correct answer.

b. Divide class into two teams. Assign a number from 1 to 10 to each pupil in each team. Teacher starts by clapping hands once, pointing to Team A and saying *One!* Pupil who was assigned number 1 claps hands, points to Team B and says *Two!* etc.

4. Let's Move.

Charades (see page 6). Teacher acts out commands from Let's Move. Pupils (individually or as class) must guess commands.

PRESENTATION

Teach pupils how to do test. Put a cassette and a marker on board rail. Ask one pupil to stand next to board. Make a statement about one of the objects.

T: *It's (a cassette).*

Pupil chooses correct object and teacher ticks board above object.

NOTE: If you want to conduct this as a formal test, go immediately to Step **1b** in Open Your Books.

OPEN YOUR BOOKS

1. Pupils open their books to page 31.

a. Play cassette. Pupils listen and point to correct picture.

1. *This is a notebook.*
2. *These are tables.*
3. *These are markers.*
4. *This is a cassette.*
5. *How many notebooks?*
   Six notebooks.
6. *Count the girls.*
   One, two, three, four. Four girls.
7. *Make a circle.*
8. *Come here.*

b. Play cassette again. Each pupil does exercise as a written test.

2. Correct test with pupils.

1.		✓
2.		✓
3.		✓
4.	✓	
5.		✓
6.	✓	
7.	✓	
8.		✓

EXTENSION

1. Divide class into two teams and give each team a group of objects (including multiples). The first pupil from Team A holds up object(s) and asks *What's this?* or *What are these?* The corresponding pupil from Team B answers. Award one point for correctly formed questions and for correct answers.

WORKBOOK page 31

- Pupils circle correct word next to each picture. (**Answers:** *this, these, this.*)
- Pupils circle correct word. (**Answers:** *this, these.*) Then they write this word in blank and trace dotted words.
- Pupils circle correct number. (**Answers:** *two, four, eight.*) Then they write this number in blank and trace dotted words.

Unit Four

Let's Talk

LANGUAGE PATTERNS: I'm home. This is my (mother). It's nice to meet you. It's nice to meet you, too.

NEW VOCABULARY: mother

MATERIALS: squares of coloured paper—three of each colour; sets of teacher-made cards for 'Living Sentences' (extension 2); tape-recorder and cassette

REVIEW

1. Practise self-introductions from Unit 1 using **Conversation Lines** (see page 6). P1: *Hello, I am (Kate).* P2: *Hi. My name is (John).*

2. In groups of three, pupils practise greetings from Unit 3, using own names. P1: *Hi, (John). This is my friend, (Sarah).* P2: *Hi, (Sarah).*

PRESENTATION

1. Present pattern.

a. Two pupils come to front of class and stand with teacher. Introduce them to each other, using gestures. Whisper their lines to prompt them.

T: *This is my friend, (P1). This is my friend, (P2).*
P1: *It's nice to meet you.*
P2: *It's nice to meet you, too.* (Pupils should shake hands.)

b. Repeat with several other pairs of pupils.

2. Practise.
In **Conversation Lines** (see page 6), pupils practise introducing themselves.

P1: *Hello. I am (Kate).*
P2: *Hi! My name is (John).*
P1: *It's nice to meet you.*
P2: *It's nice to meet you, too.* (Pupils should shake hands.)

OPEN YOUR BOOKS

Open your Pupil's Book to page 32 and show it to pupils. Point to Kate's mother. Teach pupils word *mother.* Pupils repeat several times. Then ask pupils to name the other characters. (Option: Pupils say, in own language, what they think picture is about.)

1. Pupils open their books to page 32.

a. Play cassette. Pupils listen and point to character who is speaking.

Kate: *Hi, Mum! I'm home. This is my friend, Andy. This is my mother.*
Andy: *It's nice to meet you, Mrs. Hill.*
Mrs. Hill: *It's nice to meet you, too, Andy.*

b. Play cassette again, stopping after each line. Pupils repeat line.

2. Present sample structure and contraction.

a. Write structure on board. Read it aloud, pointing to words. Pupils repeat.
b. Write explanation of contraction on board: *It is = It's.*
c. Pupils practise *It's nice to meet you.*

NOTE: Native speakers of English always use contracted form *It's nice to meet you.*

3. Practise.
Divide class into groups of three. Pupils practise conversation using own names.

P1: *This is (John). This is (Sarah).*
P2: *It's nice to meet you.*
P3: *It's nice to meet you, too.*

Do this three times with each group, so that each pupil says all lines.

EXTENSION

1. Find Your Partners (see page 6). Give each pupil a square of coloured paper. There should be three squares of each colour. Teacher holds up one square of coloured paper and says (*Red*). Pupils holding red squares stand up and greet each other, using own names. Continue with other colours. **NOTE:** If class number can't be divided by three, teacher should also take coloured square(s) and say line(s).

2. Living Sentences (see page 7). Use the four sentences *This is my friend, This is my mother, It's nice to meet you,* and *It's nice to meet you, too.* Divide class into groups. Each group should have same number of pupils as there are words in each sentence. Give each pupil a card with a word from the sentences above written on it. Pupils arrange themselves in correct order for each sentence. They are not allowed to speak except to repeat their word. When pupils think they are standing in the correct order, they repeat their sentence for teacher. Teacher says *Yes* if everything is correct. If a pupil is in the wrong place, teacher says *No,* but does not correct the sentence at first. Give pupils another chance to find the error on their own. **NOTE:** If class can't be divided into appropriate numbers, select a small group for each sentence in turn. Some pupils may take part in more than one sentence.

WORKBOOK page 35

- Pupils name characters and trace words in speech bubbles. Then they practise question and answer pattern.
- Pupils draw pictures of their family in frame and trace sentence.

Let's Sing

LANGUAGE PATTERNS: Nice to meet you. Nice to meet you, too.

NEW VOCABULARY: father, sister, brother

MATERIALS: magazine pictures or teacher-made cards with pictures of mother, father, sister, brother (these can be copied from Pupil's Book page 35); tape-recorder and cassette; photographs of pupils' own families

REVIEW

1. Sing 'This Is My Friend'. Sing the song once for review. Then divide class into groups of 4–6 and assign characters of Sarah and John to two pupils in each group. The remaining 2–4 pupils in group are friends. Sing the song again. Groups act out roles of Sarah, John, and their friends as they sing.
2. In pairs, pupils greet each other. P1: *Hello, (Kate). It's nice to meet you.* P2: *It's nice to meet you, too.*

PRESENTATION

1. Present new vocabulary.
Use magazine pictures or teacher-made cards (of mother, father, sister, brother) to introduce new words, one at a time. Pupils repeat each word several times.

2. Practise.
Teacher holds up a family member picture and points to P1 who says *This is my (mother).* Teacher holds up another picture and points to P2 who says *This is my (sister),* etc.

OPEN YOUR BOOKS

Open your Pupil's Book to page 33. Show it to pupils and ask them to name the characters. (Option: Pupils say, in own language, what they think each picture is about.)

1. Pupils open their books to page 33.
a. Play cassette. Pupils listen and point to the family member Kate is introducing.

Kate: *This is my mother*
All: *Nice to meet you.*
Mother: *Nice to meet you, too.*

Kate: *This is my father.*
All: *Nice to meet you.*
Father: *Nice to meet you, too.*

Kate: *This is my sister.*
All: *Nice to meet you.*
Sister: *Nice to meet you, too.*

Kate: *This is my brother.*
All: *Nice to meet you.*
Brother: *Nice to meet you, too.*

b. Play cassette again. Pupils sing along.

2. Practise.
a. Divide class into three groups and sing the song again with cassette.

Group A: *This is my mother/father/sister/brother.*
Group B: *Nice to meet you.*
Group C: *Nice to meet you, too.*

b. Divide class into groups of five, each pupil taking the part of either Kate or one of the members of her family. (**NOTE:** If class number cannot be divided by 5, simply divide whole class into five groups each containing any number of pupils. Whole group will then play one part.) Pupils act out introductions as they sing.

EXTENSION

1. Practise introductions and greetings. Play 'The Family Song'. When teacher stops music and points to a pair of pupils, the pair introduce themselves, and greet each other. P1: *Hi! My name is (John).* P2: *I'm (Kate).* P1: *Nice to meet you.* P2: *Nice to meet you, too.*

2. Ask pupils to bring photographs of their families to class. Divide pupils into small groups or pairs. Pupils use pictures to introduce their family members to each other. Teacher should circulate, helping as necessary.

Let's Learn

LANGUAGE PATTERNS: Who's she/he? (She's) my (grandmother).

NEW VOCABULARY: grandmother, grandfather, baby sister, she, he

MATERIALS: two puppets or soft toys; magazine pictures or teacher-made cards of mother, father, sister, brother, grandmother, grandfather, baby sister; tape-recorder and cassette

REVIEW

1. Sing 'The Family Song'. Sing the song once for review. Then sing the song again with individual pupils taking parts of mother, father, etc.

2. Vocabulary drill. Use magazine pictures/teacher-made cards of father, mother, sister, and brother to cue pupils.

PRESENTATION

1. Present new vocabulary.
a. Use magazine pictures/teacher-made cards of grandfather, grandmother, and baby sister to introduce new words. Pupils repeat each word several times.
b. Use pictures/teacher-made cards to practise names of all family members. Class stands. Show them one picture card. Say name of a family member. Pupils remain standing if teacher uses correct name. They sit down if teacher is incorrect.

T: (Show 'father' card.) *Father.* (Pupils remain standing.)
T: *Mother.* (Pupils sit down.)

2. Present pattern.
a. Place pictures/teacher-made cards of grandfather and grandmother on board rail. Use puppets to model question and answer.

Puppet A: *Who's she?*
Puppet B: *She's my grandmother.*
Puppet A: *Who's he?*
Puppet B: *He's my grandfather.*

Puppets point to pictures as they speak.

b. Pupils repeat each line, three times, in chorus, after each question and answer.
c. Repeat Steps **a** and **b** for remaining family members.

3. Practise.
Divide class into two groups. Use family member pictures/cards to cue groups.

Group A: *Who's (she)?*
Group B: *(She's) my (grandmother).*

After Group A finishes, Group B asks Group A the questions.

OPEN YOUR BOOKS

Open your Pupil's Book to page 34. Show it to pupils and ask them to name the characters. (Option: Pupils say, in own language, what they think characters are saying.)

1. Pupils open their books to page 34.
a. Play cassette. Pupils listen and point to character who is speaking.

Andy: *Who's she?*
Kate: *She's my grandmother.*
Andy: *Who's he?*
Kate: *He's my grandfather.*

b. Play cassette again, stopping after each line. Pupils repeat line.

2. Present sample structures and contraction.
a. Write structures on board. Read them aloud, pointing to words. Pupils repeat.
b. Write explanations of contractions on board:
Who is = Who's
She is = She's
He is = He's

c. Pupils practise *Who is she/he?, Who's she/he?, She is my grandmother,* and *She's my grandmother,* etc. Point to explanation on board as you practise.

3. Practise.
Divide class into two groups. Practise question and answer pattern with new vocabulary on PB page 35, using girl and boy as models. Half of class is girl and other half is boy. Then reverse roles.

4. Look at activity at bottom of page 35. In pairs, pupils point to pictures and make sentences following model. Teacher should circulate, helping as necessary.

EXTENSION

1. Pupils draw pictures of their own families. Ask pupil volunteers, in turn, to come to front of class with one picture. Class asks *Who's (he)?* P1 answers *(He's) my (father).*

(Continued on page 41.)

WORKBOOK pages 36 and 37

page 36

- Pupils trace names of family members and practise question and answer pattern.
- Pupils circle correct pronoun next to each picture. (**Answers**: *she, he, she.*)

page 37

- Pupils trace sample question. Then, inside each speech bubble, they write appropriate question for each answer. (**Answers**: *Who's she? Who's she? Who's he?*)
- Pupils trace sample labels. Then they trace and write a correct label for each picture. (**Answers**: *grandmother, father, mother, brother, sister.*)
- Pupils draw a line from each question to matching answer. (**Answers**: *Who's she? She's my sister. / What's this? It's a fish. / What are these? They're crayons.)*

Let's Learn Some More

LANGUAGE PATTERNS: (He's) (tall). (She's) (short).

NEW VOCABULARY: tall, short, young, old, pretty, ugly, fat, thin

MATERIALS: magazine pictures or teacher-made cards for family members; magazine pictures (several of each) to illustrate adjectives; tape-recorder and cassette

REVIEW

1. Sing 'The Family Song'. Choose four pupils to be family members.

2. Divide class into two teams. Hold up one family member picture/card. Team A says *(He's) my father.* Award a point for correct answer. Then show another card to Team B, etc.

PRESENTATION

1. Present new vocabulary.
a. Draw pictures on board to illustrate pairs of adjectives (tall/short, young/old, pretty/ugly, fat/thin). Use clear physical gestures to contrast meanings of adjectives. Pupils repeat each word several times. After introducing each pair of adjectives (example: *tall/short*) conduct a quick mini-drill.
b. The Right Choice (see page 7). Divide class into two teams. Use board drawings of adjectives to cue teams. One pupil from each team, in turn, goes up and stands by board. Teacher says an adjective and pupil points to drawing. Award a point for correct choice.

2. Present pattern.
a. Point to drawing on board of tall person. T: *(He's) tall.* Point to drawing of short person. T: *(She's) short.*
b. Pupils repeat three times.
c. Follow Steps **a** and **b** for *young/old, pretty/ugly,* and *fat/thin.*

3. Practise.
Distribute magazine pictures illustrating adjectives. T: *(He's) short.* Pupil(s) with appropriate pictures(s) hold(s) it/them up.

OPEN YOUR BOOKS

Open your Pupil's Book to page 36. Show it to pupils and ask them to name the character (Kate).

1. Pupils open their books to page 36.
a. Play cassette. Pupils listen and point to pictures of tall man and short girl respectively.

Kate: *He's tall. She's short.*

b. Play cassette again, stopping after each sentence. Pupils repeat sentence, pointing to picture.

2. Present sample structures and contractions.
a. Write structures on board. Read them aloud, pointing to words. Pupils repeat.
b. Write explanation of contractions on board:
He is = He's
She is = She's
c. Pupils practise *He is tall, He's tall, She is short, She's short.*

3. Practise.
Look at practice activity on PB pages 36 and 37.
a. Describe each of the pictures at bottom of page 36. Pupils point to pictures and repeat.
b. Read each riddle aloud (page 37). Repeat riddle several times and ask a pupil to guess which person is being described. P1: *She's my (grandmother).* (**Answers**: *grandmother, brother, grandfather, baby sister.*)

EXTENSION

1. Memory Chain (see page 7). Divide class into two or three teams. In turn, each team tries to make chain as long as possible without forgetting any items. Each pupil in team adds one item to chain.

P1: *(She's) (short).*
P2: *(She's) (short)* and *(she's) (pretty).*

WORKBOOK pages 38 and 39

page 38

- Pupils draw a line from each picture to one showing its opposite. (**Answers**: *fat — thin / ugly — pretty.*) Then they trace adjectives under pictures.
- Pupils circle correct adjective next to each picture. (**Answers**: *tall, young, pretty, fat.*) They write these adjectives in blanks. Then they trace remaining words in sentences.

page 39

- Pupils trace sample label and then complete other labels for pictures. (**Answers**: *book, cat, desk, egg, fish.*)
- Pupils trace words. Then they write a sentence for each picture, using an adjective from list. (**Answers**: *She's pretty. He's ugly. He's thin. She's old. He's fat.)*

ABC abc Let's Learn the Alphabet

NEW VOCABULARY: house, ink, jeans

MATERIALS: tape-recorder and cassette; lined paper

1. Review letters *A–F*. Assign a letter *A–F* to each pupil. All pupils must recite the alphabet from A to F. As each pupil's letter is called, pupil must stand up.

2. Pupils open their books to bottom of page 37.

a. Play cassette. Pupils listen and point to letters.

Teacher: *G, girl; H, house; I, ink; J, jeans.*

b. Play cassette again, stopping after each letter. Pupils repeat letter and word.

c. Say word *girl* carefully, emphasizing initial sound. Print word *girl* on board and underline *g*.

d. Put letter *g* next to word *girl* on board.

g—girl

Ask pupils to think of other words that begin with the same sound (e.g. *grandmother*).

e. Repeat Steps **c** and **d** for words *house, ink,* and *jeans*.

3. Show pupils how to print small *g*. Then introduce capital *G*. Repeat for letters *H, I,* and *J*. Practise printing letters on lined paper.

WORKBOOK page 40

- Pupils trace name under each picture.
- Pupils circle letter that name of each picture begins with. (**Answers**: *i, J, g*.) Then they write these letters in blanks under each picture.

Let's Move

LANGUAGE PATTERNS: (Don't) go to sleep, wake up, do your homework, eat your dinner, make a mess, tidy up, watch TV, play the piano

NEW VOCABULARY: good night, good morning, sleep, wake up, homework, mess, tidy, watch TV, piano, dinner

MATERIALS: tape-recorder and cassette; slips of paper each with a tick or a cross (one per pupil)

REVIEW

Review commands from Unit 3. Ask appropriate number of pupils to do each command. Class repeats command.

PRESENTATION

1. Present commands.
a. Model command phrases using clear gestures.
b. Say commands. Pupils listen and do commands.
c. Repeat commands. Pupils listen, repeat, and do commands.
d. Divide class into two groups and practise commands as in previous units.

2. Play a game.
Charades (see page 6). Teacher mimes commands. Pupils guess.

OPEN YOUR BOOKS

Open your Pupil's Book to page 38 and show it to pupils. Point to each picture in turn and say command. Pupils repeat and mime command.

1. Pupils open their books to page 38.
a. Play cassette, omitting negative commands. Pupils listen and point to each action.

Go to sleep. (Good night)!
Wake up. (Good morning)!
Do your homework.
Eat your dinner.
Make a mess.
Tidy up.
Watch TV.
Play the piano.

b. Play cassette again, stopping after each command. Pupils say command.

2. Say commands in random order, stopping after each one. Pupils point to correct picture and repeat command.

3. Each pupil, in turn, points to a picture and gives command (with teacher's help). Class repeats and does command.

4. Present sample structure and contraction.
a. Write structure on board. Read it aloud, pointing to words. Pupils repeat. Then draw two simple outlines of television sets on board. Put a cross through one of them. Point to first picture and say *Watch TV.* Then point to crossed-out picture and say *Don't watch TV.* Pupils repeat.
b. Write explanation of contraction on board: *Do not = Don't.*
c. Pupils practise *Do not watch TV* and *Don't watch TV.*
d. Play cassette (negative commands only), stopping after each command. Pupils repeat command.

Don't watch TV.
Don't make a mess.

e. Pupils repeat pattern, using *don't* for remaining commands. Use pictures on PB page 38 to cue pupils.

EXTENSION

1. Pupils all stand. Teacher says *Play the piano.* Pupils pretend to play piano and continue until teacher says *Don't play the piano.* Then pupils stop. Teacher should repeat command every few seconds while pupils are acting out command, and then randomly insert negative command.

2. Hand out slips of paper with ticks/crosses on them (one per pupil). Divide class into two groups. Each pupil from Group A, in turn, gives either a positive or a negative command to Group B, depending on whether her/his paper has a tick or a cross. Group B mimes action or does nothing. Reverse roles and repeat.

WORKBOOK page 41

- Pupils draw a line from each command to matching picture. Then they trace commands.
- Pupils trace words under pictures.

Let's Listen

LANGUAGE PATTERNS: Unit review

VOCABULARY: Unit review

MATERIALS: magazine pictures or teacher-made cards of family members; tape-recorder and cassette; big sheets of paper for family trees

REVIEW

1. Let's Talk.
Role play. Ask pupil volunteers to go to front of class in groups of three and act out dialogue

2. Let's Learn.
Tic Tac Toe (see page 7). Use pictures/teacher-made cards of family members. Divide class into two teams, X and O. Point to a picture. T: *Who's (she)?* P1: *She's my (grandmother).* Correct answers earn team an X or O on grid.

3. Let's Learn Some More.
Draw pictures showing pairs of adjectives on board. Ask pupil volunteer to go to board and point to a picture. Class answers *(She's) (old).* Continue with other volunteers.

4. Let's Move.
Pupils mime commands as teacher says them. Teacher should use all of the commands in both positive and negative *(don't)* forms (for sixteen possibilities). Teacher should give commands at random (For example: *Go to sleep. Do your homework. Don't do your homework. Play the piano.*) Also, review previous commands from Units 1–3 with *don't.*

OPEN YOUR BOOKS

1. Pupils open their books to page 39.
a. Play cassette. Pupils listen and point to correct picture

1. *She's my mother.*
2. *He's my grandfather.*
3. *Who's she?*
   She's my baby sister.
4. *Who's he?*
   He's my father.
5. *He's tall.*
6. *She's pretty.*
7. *Tidy up.*
8. *Don't watch TV.*

b. Play cassette again. Each pupil does exercise as a written test.

2. Correct tests with pupils.

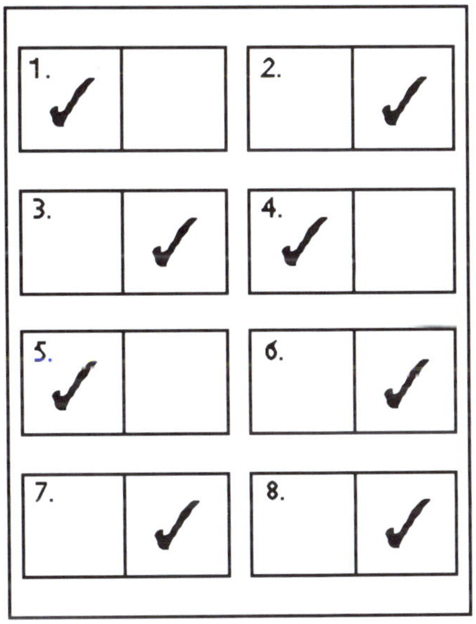

EXTENSION

1. Pupils draw own family trees, labelling each picture *mother, brother,* etc. Then, in pairs, they explain their trees to each other.
P1 points to picture on P2's tree: *Who's (he)?* P2: *(He's) my (brother).*

WORKBOOK page 42

- Pupils circle sentence that describes each picture. (**Answers**: *He is ugly. She is old. She is short.*) Then they trace sentences.
- Pupils draw a line from each female family member to her male counterpart. (**Answers**: *grandfather — grandmother / mother — father.)* Then they trace words.

Let's Review

LANGUAGE PATTERNS: General review

VOCABULARY: General review

MATERIALS: realia or pictures of classroom objects (singles and multiples): crayon(s), pencil case(s), cassette(s), table(s), marker(s), notebook(s); pupil's family photographs; sets of dice; tape-recorder and cassette

REVIEW

1. Songs.

a. Sing 'This is My Friend' and 'The Family Song' as a whole class.
b. Pupils, in groups of three, come to front of class to introduce each other, practising informal introductions from Unit 4.

P1: *Hi, (Amy). This is my friend, (Sue).*
P2: *Hello, (Sue).*
P3: *Hi, (Amy).*

c. Repeat practice, this time with groups of three introducing each other with formal introductions from Unit 4.

P1: *Hello, (Miss Lee).*
T: *Hello, (Amy).*
P1: *This is my friend, (Sue). This is my teacher.*
T: *It's nice to meet you.*
P2: *It's nice to meet you, too.*

2. Vocabulary.

a. Use realia/pictures of classroom objects. Quickly show three and name the objects (some singular and some plural). Then hold up one group/object at a time. Pupils must name correctly.
b. Pupils bring in photographs of their own families or use family tree drawings made for Unit 4. Pupil volunteers introduce and describe their family members to class. *This is my (mother). (She's) (tall).* (Use family on page 35 of Pupil's Book for pupils who have no pictures.)

3. Structures.

a. Draw single and multiple pictures of classroom objects on board. Ask each pupil, in turn, to name a picture, using a full sentence. *This is (a table). These are (crayons).*
b. Divide class into three teams A, B, and C. Team A comes to front of room and pupils stand side-by-side. Teacher points to first pupil in Team A. One pupil from Team B must ask *Who's she?* or *Who's he?* A pupil from Team C must answer *He's (John)* or *She's (Mary)*. A correct question or answer earns team a point. When all pupils in Team A have been identified, rotate two more times so that Teams A and C both ask questions.
c. Divide class into pairs and give each pair the name of a classroom object. Pair must count all those they can find on or near their desks, including objects in their bags. Then each pair reports what they found to class.

T: *(Crayon).*
Class: *How many (crayons)?*
Pair 1: *(Six) (crayons).*

4. Commands.
Do a quick review of Unit 3 and 4 commands, including *don't* phrases. Teacher gives commands to small groups of pupils to mime.

OPEN YOUR BOOKS

1. Say these.
Pupils open their books to page 40. Teacher circulates as pupils do the following activities.

a. Pupils review vocabulary by pointing to each picture in order, and calling out name of picture, in chorus. (**Answers**: *a cassette, cassettes, a marker, markers, a table, tables, a boy, boys, a girl, girls.*)
b. Divide class into pairs. Give each pair a dice. Pupils take turns rolling the dice, moving number of spaces equal to number on the dice, and identifying picture. Pupils continue game until one pupil lands directly on goal.
c. Divide class into pairs. P1 identifies all picture cues as quickly as possible. P2 listens and helps P1 if necessary. If all pictures are identified correctly, P1 receives 10 points. Reverse roles and play again.

2. Ask your partner.
Divide class into two groups. Practise question and answer pattern at bottom of page 40, using boy and girl as models. Both groups should ask and answer questions.

3. Say and act.

a. Look at pictures at top of PB page 41. Point to first blank speech bubble and say *Hello, Sarah.* Point to second blank speech bubble and ask pupils to guess what should be there. (**Answer**: *Hi, John. This is my friend, Sarah.*) Repeat for second picture. (**Answer**: *(It's) Nice to meet you, too.)*
b. In pairs, pupils practise both dialogues. Teacher should circulate, helping as necessary.

4. Answer the question.
Divide class into two groups and look at picture cues in middle of page 41. Group A asks *How many (crayons)?* Group B counts aloud and then answers: *(Eight) (crayons)*. Repeat, reversing roles.

5. Listen carefully.

a. Play cassette. Pupils listen and point to correct picture.

a: *Play the piano.*
b. *Don't go to the door.*

(Continued on page 47.)

b. Play cassette again. Pupils listen and tick small box next to correct answer.

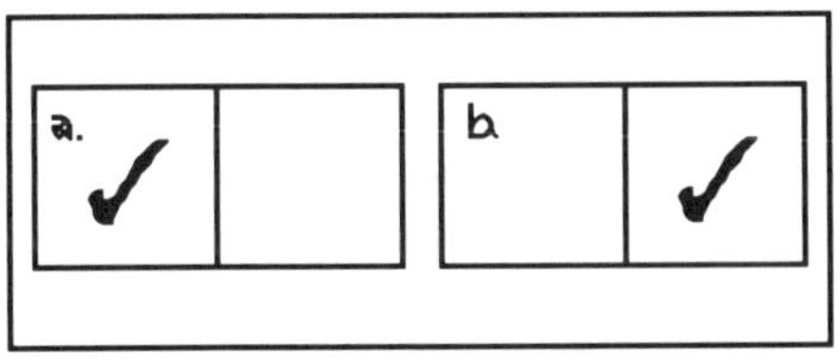

c. Pupils identify other two pictures and say commands. (*Don't play the piano. Go to the door.*) Then they say all four commands.

EXTENSION

1. Give class variations on commands. T: *Make two circles. Go to the desk. Give me an eraser. Count the books. Count the girls*, etc. Class repeats command and does or mimes action.

WORKBOOK pages 43 and 44

page 43

- Pupils write names of items in squares (one letter per square) to complete crossword puzzle. (**Answers**: 1 *fish*, 2 *jeans*, 3 *house*, 4 *egg*, 5 *girl*, 6 *ink*, 7 *desk*.)
- Pupils circle correct pronoun next to each picture. (**Answers**: *he, she, she, he*.)

page 44

- Pupils trace words. Then they draw a line from each word to matching number.
- Pupils write correct adjective in each sentence. (**Answers**: *He is old. She is young. She is tall. He is short.*)

Unit Five

Let's Talk

LANGUAGE PATTERNS: Happy Birthday, (Jenny). How old are you? I'm (seven) years old. This is for you. Wow! A (robot). Thank you.

NEW VOCABULARY: robot, Happy Birthday, thank you

MATERIALS: magazine pictures showing a variety of young/old, tall/short, pretty/ugly, fat/thin people; teacher-made card of robot—placed inside small box (can be traced from Pupil's Book page 45); two puppets or soft toys; tape-recorder and cassette; grids (one per pupil) for Bingo

REVIEW

1. Charades (see page 6). Ask for pupil volunteers. Whisper a command from Pupil's Book page 38 to each pupil in turn. Pupil acts out command and class guesses.

2. Give each pupil a magazine picture illustrating adjective. Teacher or volunteer says (*Thin*). Pupils with pictures of thin people hold them up. Each pupil says *(He's) (thin)*. Continue with other adjectives.

PRESENTATION

1. Present first part of dialogue.
  a. Puppet A: (Humming 'Happy Birthday to You', carrying a small box as a gift, meets Puppet B.) *Happy Birthday, (Kate)!*
  Puppet B: *Thank you.*
  Puppet A: *How old are you?*
  Puppet B: *I'm seven years old.*
  b. Pupils repeat each line of dialogue three times, in chorus.

2. Present complete dialogue.

Puppet A: (Humming 'Happy Birthday to You' and carrying a small box as a gift, meets Puppet B.) *Happy Birthday,(Kate)! How old are you?*
Puppet B: *I'm seven years old.*
Puppet A: *This is for you.* (Gives box to Puppet B.)
Puppet B: (Opening box and taking out robot card.) *Wow! A robot! Thank you!*

Pupils repeat each line of dialogue three times, in chorus.

3. Practise.
Divide class into two groups and practise dialogue.

OPEN YOUR BOOKS

Open your Pupil's Book to page 42. Show it to pupils and ask them to name the characters. (Option: Pupils say, in own language, what they think each picture is about.)

1. Pupils open their books to page 42.
  a. Play cassette. Pupils listen and point to character(s) who is/are speaking.

  Lisa: *Happy birthday, Jenny!*
  John: *How old are you?*
  Jenny: *I'm seven years old.*
  Lisa & John: *This is for you.*
  Jenny: *Wow! A robot! Thank you!*

  b. Play cassette again, stopping after each line. Pupils repeat line.

2. Present sample structures and contraction.
  a. Write structures on board. Read them aloud, pointing to words. Pupils repeat.
  b. Write explanation of contraction on board: *I am = I'm.*
  c. Pupils practise *I am seven years old* and *I'm seven years old.*

3. Practise.
  a. Divide class into two groups and practise dialogue (from Presentation **1a)** using contracted form.
  b. Pupils continue practising dialogue in pairs. For gifts, pupils can give their partners classroom objects wrapped in paper.

EXTENSION

1. Tic Tac Toe (see page 7). Divide class into two or more teams. Take questions from Units 1–4 and Unit 5 Let's Talk. Ask pupils from each team questions. Correct answers earn team an X or O on grid drawn on board.

2. Bingo (see page 6) with colours, numbers, and letters. Give each pupil a blank grid with nine squares drawn on it, or ask pupils to draw their own grid following teacher's model. At random, each pupil colours three squares, writes a number in three squares, and a letter in three squares. Teacher or volunteer pupil calls out a colour, number, or letter. If it appears on their cards, pupils cross it out.

WORKBOOK page 45

- Pupils count candles on each cake and write number in blank. (**Answers**: *8, 7.*)
- Pupils trace words in sentence. Then they write own ages (in letters) in blank. Then they draw same numbers of candles on cake. Then they practise question and answer pattern.

Let's Sing

LANGUAGE PATTERNS: It's my/your birthday today.

MATERIALS: miscellaneous classroom objects; two puppets or soft toys; birthday hat or some birthday-related realia (small cake, for example); tape-recorder and cassette; beanbag or ball

REVIEW

1. Sing 'The Family Song' with cassette. Divide class into five groups, representing narrator, father, mother, sister, and brother. Teacher is friend who will meet family. (Numbers in each group don't matter.) Pupils should use gestures, waves, etc. as they sing their parts.

2. Divide class into pairs. Give each pupil a classroom object (pencil, notebook, eraser, etc.). Pupils practise dialogue from Unit 5, Let's Talk using own names and ages. They give each other objects as gifts.

PRESENTATION

1. Present first pattern, using the possessive adjectives *my* and *your.*

a. Use puppets to model *my* and *your.*

Puppet A: (Presenting small cake to Puppet B.) *It's your birthday today.* (Emphasize *your.*)
Puppet B: *Yes, it's my birthday today.* (Emphasize *my.*)
(Puppet who is speaking should point to self or other puppet to indicate *my* or *your.*)

b. Ask a pupil volunteer to come to front. Give pupil a birthday hat to wear, or a cake or some other object to indicate a birthday.

T: *It's your birthday today.* (Pointing to pupil.)
P1: *It's my birthday today.* (Pointing to self.)

Then P1 chooses P2 to come up, and gives the same gift to P2.

P1: *It's your birthday today.*
P2: *It's my birthday today.*

Repeat with one or two more pupils.

2. Present second pattern.

a. Use puppets to model pattern.

Puppet A: (Drawing a birthday cake with seven candles on board.) *I'm seven years old.*
Puppet B: *You're seven years old.*

Pupils repeat three times, in chorus.

b. Ask two pupil volunteers to come to front. Draw another birthday cake next to first one but without candles. P1 draws candles on cake to indicate P1's age.

P1: *I'm (eight) years old.*
P2: *You're (eight) years old.*

Repeat with other pairs of pupils.

c. Pupils practise last pattern using **Conversation Lines** (see page 6).

OPEN YOUR BOOKS

Open your Pupil's Book to page 43 and show it to pupils. Ask them to name the characters and say whose birthday it is (Jenny's)

1. Pupils open their books to page 43.

a. Play cassette.

It's my birthday today.
It's your birthday today.
It's my birthday today.
Happy birthday, Jenny!

One, two, three, four, five, six,
Seven years old!

Now I'm seven years old.
Now you're seven years old.
Now I'm seven years old.
Happy birthday, Jenny!

b. Play cassette again. Pupils sing along.

2. Practise.

a. Divide class into two groups and sing the song again with cassette, using gestures to indicate *my* and *your.*

Group A: *It's my birthday today.*
Group B: *It's your birthday today.*
Group A: *It's my birthday today.*
Group B: *Happy birthday, Jenny!*
All: *One, two, three, four, five, six, seven years old!*
Group A: *Now I'm seven years old.*
Group B: *Now you're seven years old.*
Group A: *Now I'm seven years old.*
Group B: *Happy birthday, Jenny.*

b. Sing the song again, with pupil volunteers taking solo parts and whole class singing chorus.

EXTENSION

1. Beanbag Game (see page 6). P1 tosses beanbag or ball to P2 and asks *How old are you?* P2 answers *I'm (eight) years old.* All: *Happy Birthday, (Tommy).* Then P2 tosses beanbag to P3.

2. Display a large calendar, or draw a large calendar on board with name of month and days of week deleted. Give each pupil a piece of paper with a number corresponding to a date on calendar. Touch one date on calendar. Pupil holding that date stands up.
P: *It's my birthday today.* The others respond. Ps: *Happy birthday!* Repeat with several different birthdays. Afterwards fill in pupils' real birthdays on calendar.

Let's Learn

LANGUAGE PATTERNS: What is it? I don't know. It's (a doll).

NEW VOCABULARY: a yo-yo, a car, a doll, a robot, a racket, a kite, a ball, a puzzle, a skipping rope, a bicycle

MATERIALS: wrapped package with a small doll inside (provided by the teacher); two puppets or soft toy animals; tape-recorder and cassette

REVIEW

1. Divide class into two groups to identify and describe family members. Use page 39 of Pupil's Book to cue pupils. Group A (pointing to first picture): *Who's she?* Group B: *She's my mother.* After each question and answer, ask a pupil volunteer to make a sentence about the picture, using an adjective. P1: *She's (pretty).* For second picture reverse roles.

PRESENTATION

1. Present new vocabulary.
a. Make simple board drawings to introduce new words, one at a time. Pupils repeat several times. After each new word, conduct a quick mini-drill, alternating new word with previously introduced words.
b. Drill new vocabulary.

T: *What's this?*
Ps: *It's (a doll).*

2. Present pattern.
a. Place a wrapped package containing small doll in front of Puppet B and model first question and answer.

Puppet A: *What is it?*
Puppet B: *I don't know.*

Pupils repeat each line of dialogue three times, in chorus.
b. Unwrap package and model second question and answer.

Puppet A: *What is it?*
Puppet B: *It's a doll.*

Pupils repeat each line of dialogue three times, in chorus.
c. Ask *What is it?* for the remaining vocabulary words. Point to drawings on board.

T: *What is it?*
Ps: *It's (a yo-yo).*

3. Practise.
Divide class into two teams. A pupil from Team A comes to front, points to a drawing on board, and asks *What is it?* Team B: *It's (a yo-yo).* Then a pupil from Team B asks a question. Award points for correct questions and answers.

OPEN YOUR BOOKS

Open your Pupil's Book to page 44. Show it to pupils and ask them to name the characters. (Option: Pupils say, in own language, what they think each picture is about.)

1. Pupils open their books to page 44.
a. Play cassette. Pupils listen and point to character who is speaking.

Scott: *What is it?*
Jenny: *I don't know.*
Scott: *What is it?*
Jenny: *It's a doll.*

b. Play cassette again, stopping after each line. Pupils repeat line.

2. Present sample structures and contraction.
a. Write structures on board. Read them aloud, pointing to words. Pupils repeat.
b. Write explanation of contraction on board: *It is = It's.*
c. Pupils practise *It is a doll* and *It's a doll.*

3. Practise.
a. Divide class into two groups. Practise question and answer pattern with new vocabulary on PB page 45, using cats as models.
b. In pairs, pupils continue question and answer practice.

4. Look at activity at bottom of page 45. Divide class into pairs. In turn, each pair looks at a wrapped present and one pupil guesses what it is. P1 points to one present. P1: *What is it?* P2: *It's (a doll)* or *I don't know.* When all pairs have finished, repeat practice starting with last pair. P2 should ask question.

EXTENSION

1. Bingo (see page 6). Each pupil draws objects (from new vocabulary) in three squares, colours three squares, and writes letters in three squares.

WORKBOOK pages 46 and 47

page 46
- Pupils trace labels.
- Pupils trace words. Then they complete sentences. (**Answers**: *It is a ball. It is a kite. It is a car. It is a doll.*) Then they practise question and answer pattern.

page 47
- Pupils trace words. Then they complete a question and answer for each picture. (**Answers**: *How old are you? I'm ten. / How old are you? I'm nine. / How old are you? I'm eight.*)
- Pupils trace words. Then they complete sentences to match pictures. (**Answers**: *It's a kite. It's a bicycle. It's a robot. It's a yo-yo. It's a racket. It's a doll.*)

Let's Learn Some More

LANGUAGE PATTERNS: It's (little). Is it (a yo-yo)? No, it isn't. Yes, it is. It's (a little yo-yo).

NEW VOCABULARY: little, big, long, short, round, square

MATERIALS: yo-yo; two puppets or soft toys; tape-recorder and cassette

REVIEW

1. Sing 'The Happy Birthday Song'. Divide class into two groups and assign each group a part of song.

2. Quickly review Let's Learn vocabulary, using pictures on PB page 45. Class asks *What is it?* for each object. Pupils answer in turn *It's (a yo-yo).*

PRESENTATION

1. Present new vocabulary.
a. On board, draw objects to introduce new pairs of adjectives (e.g. little and big fish, long and short pencils, round and square boxes). Pupils repeat each word several times. After introducing each new word, conduct a quick mini-drill, alternating new word with previously introduced words.
b. Point to drawings in random order and ask pupils to say adjectives. Ps: *It's (little).* Repeat for remaining adjectives.

2. Present pattern.
a. Place yo-yo on board rail. Use puppets to model pattern. Hold puppets so that only Puppet A can 'see' yo-yo.

Puppet A: *It's little. What is it?*
Puppet B: *Is it a ball?*
Puppet A: *No, it isn't.*
Puppet B: *Is it a yo-yo?*
Puppet A: *Yes, it is.*

b. Pupils repeat each line of dialogue three times, in chorus, after each question and answer. Repeat pattern several times using pictures on PB page 45 and new adjectives.

3. Practise.
a. Think of an object from page 45 vocabulary. Pupils must guess what it is. T: *It's (little). What is it?* Ps: *Is it (a doll)?* T: *No, it isn't./ Yes, it is.* After pupils guess correctly, think of another object and repeat. Continue with all objects.
b. Divide class into pairs and repeat practice with each pair choosing object.

OPEN YOUR BOOKS

Open your Pupil's Book to page 46. Show it to pupils and ask them to name the characters and gifts.

1. Pupils open their books to page 46.
a. Play cassette. Pupils listen and point to character who is speaking.

Jenny: *It's little. What is it?*
Scott: *Is it a ball?*
Jenny: *No, it isn't.*
Scott: *Is it a yo-yo?*
Jenny: *Yes, it is. It's a little yo-yo.*

b. Play cassette again, stopping after each line. Pupils repeat line.

2. Present sample structures and contraction.
a. Write structures on board. Read them aloud, pointing to words. Pupils repeat.
b. Write explanation of contraction on board: *It is = It's.*
c. Pupils practise *It is little, It's little, It is a little yo-yo,* and *It's a little yo-yo.*

3. Practise.
Look at activity at bottom of page 46.
a. Model statement presented by cat. Pupils repeat.
b. Pupils make statements about boxes using picture cues. Ps: *It's (a little box).*
c. In pairs, pupils continue practice.

4. Look at activity at top of PB page 47.
a. Describe each of the objects, using full sentences. T: *It's (a long pencil).* Pupils point to object and repeat sentence.
b. Model question and answer pattern presented by cats. Pupils repeat.
c. Divide class into two groups. Each group practises asking and answering question.
d. In pairs, pupils continue practice, using picture cues in their books.

EXTENSION

1. Divide class into pairs. Teacher says pair of adjectives (e.g. *round/square*). Each pair of pupils looks for objects on their desks or in their bags to fit these adjectives. When they have found objects they put their hands up. When teacher points to pair of pupils, P1 holds object up and says *It's (long).* Class responds: *It's a (long) (pencil).* Then P2 holds up object.

2. In turns, pupil volunteers instruct class to draw objects from picture cues on PB page 47. P: *It's a long pencil.*

(Continued on page 52.)

WORKBOOK pages 48 and 49

page 48

- Pupils circle correct answers. Then they trace answers under pictures.
- Pupils circle correct answers. (**Answers**: *Yes, it is. No, it is not.*) Then they write these answers under pictures.
- Pupils circle correct adjective next to each picture. (**Answers**: *big, little.*) Then they write these adjectives in blanks and trace the words.

page 49

- Pupils trace words. Then they complete sentences using information from pictures. (**Answers**: *It's a big kite. It's a round box. It's a square box. It's a long skipping rope. It's a short skipping rope.*) Then they draw a line from each sentence to matching picture.
- Pupils draw lines between opposite adjectives. (**Answers**: *tall—short / pretty—ugly / thin—fat / big—little.*)
- Pupils trace word and letters. Then they write words beginning with each of the letters shown. (**Answers**: There is no one right word for each letter but examples of words already presented are: boy, cat, desk, egg, fish, girl, house, ink, jeans, kite, lion, marker, nine.)

Let's Learn the Alphabet

NEW VOCABULARY: lion

MATERIALS: tape-recorder and cassette; lined paper

1. Review alphabet by singing 'The Alphabet Song'.

2. Pupils open their books to bottom of page 47.

a. Play cassette. Pupils listen and point to letters.

Teacher: *K, kite; L, lion; M, mother; N, notebook.*

b. Play cassette again, stopping after each letter. Pupils repeat letter and words.
c. Say word *kite* carefully, emphasizing initial sound. Print word *kite* on board and underline *k*.
d. Print letter *k* next to word *kite* on board.

k—kite

Ask pupils to think of other words that begin with the same sound. (**NOTE:** There are no other words in this book beginning with *k*—apart from *know*—but other possibilities are *key, king, kitchen.*) Pupils may suggest words beginning with *c*. You should encourage this but write *c* and *k* words in two lists on board, pointing to difference.
e. Repeat Steps **c** and **d** for words *lion, mother,* and *notebook.*

3. Show pupils how to print a small *k*. Then introduce capital *K*. Repeat for letters *L, M,* and *N*. Practise printing letters on lined paper.

WORKBOOK page 50

- Pupils trace names of objects. Then they draw a line from each letter to object whose name begins with this letter.
- Pupils circle letter that begins each word and write this letter in blank. (**Answers**: *Kate, listen, marker, nine.*)

Let's Move

LANGUAGE PATTERNS: play with a yo-yo, kick a ball, catch a ball, hit a ball, do a puzzle, skip, Can you (play with a yo-yo?). Yes, I can. No, I can't.

VOCABULARY: kick, catch, hit, skip, puzzle

MATERIALS: tape-recorder and cassette

REVIEW

1. Divide class into groups to practise adjectives shown on PB page 36. In turn, each group looks at a pair of pictures and says e.g. *He's young. She's old.*

2. Ask pupil volunteers to give commands from Unit 4 to class. Volunteers can look at PB page 38.

PRESENTATION

1. Present commands.
  a. Model command phrases using clear gestures.
  b. Say commands. Pupils listen and mime commands.
  c. Repeat the commands. Pupils listen, repeat, and mime commands.
  d. Divide class into two groups and practise commands.

2. Play a game.
Mime commands. Pupils must guess commands.

OPEN YOUR BOOKS

Open your Pupil's Book to page 48 and show it to pupils. Point to each picture in turn and say command. Pupils repeat and mime command.

1. Pupils open their books to page 48.
  a. Play cassette, omitting dialogue. Pupils listen and point to each action.

Play with a yo-yo.
Kick a ball.
Catch a ball.
Hit a ball.
Do a puzzle.
Skip.

  b. Play cassette again, stopping after each line. Pupils repeat line.

2. Say commands in random order. Pupils point to correct picture and repeat command.

3. Each pupil, in turn, points to a picture and gives command (with teacher's help). Class repeats and mimes command.

4. Present sample structures and contraction.
  a. Write structures on board. Read them aloud, pointing to words. Pupils repeat.
  b. Write explanation of contraction on board: *cannot = can't.*
  c. Pupils practise *No, I cannot* and *No, I can't.*
  d. Play dialogue on cassette. Pupils listen and point to Scott and John respectively, at bottom of page 48.

Lisa: *Can you play with a yo-yo?*
Scott: *Yes, I can.*
John: *No, I can't.*

  e. Play cassette again, stopping after each line. Pupils repeat line.

5. Practise.
Use pictures on page 48. Point to first picture. T: *Can you play with a yo-yo?* Ps: *Yes, I can* or *No, I can't.* Repeat with other pictures.

EXTENSION

1. Please (see page 7). Divide class into small groups of any number. One group at a time comes to front of class. Teacher gives commands taken from Units 1–5. If teacher says *please* in front of command, pupils should do or mime. If teacher does not say *please,* pupils should remain still.

2. In pairs, pupils ask each other *Can you _______?* using pictures on page 48 as cues.

WORKBOOK page 51

- Pupils draw a line from each command to matching picture. Then they trace commands.
- Pupils trace answers to questions.
- Pupils write answer to question at bottom of page. Then they practise question and answer pattern.

Let's Listen

LANGUAGE PATTERNS: Unit review
VOCABULARY: Unit review
MATERIALS: yo-yo and small ball; tape-recorder and cassette

REVIEW

1. Let's Talk.
In pairs, pupils wish each other *Happy Birthday!* and practise dialogue from PB page 42. Pupils 'give' each other classroom objects as gifts. They should use own names and ages in dialogue.

2. Let's Learn.
Draw toys from Let's Learn on board. In turn, each pupil says *It's (a doll)* as teacher points to object.

3. Let's Learn Some More.
Divide class into two teams. Use board drawings of toys to cue pupils. Point to a drawing. T: *It's a doll.* One pupil from Team A uses object in sentence with adjective. P1: *It's a (big) (doll).* Award team one point for each correct sentence.

4. Let's Move.
a. Quickly give class commands to do or mime.
b. Play **Please** (see page 7) with volunteer leaders. Leaders can look at pictures on PB page 48.

PRESENTATION

Teach pupils how to do test. Put a yo-yo and a small ball on board rail. Ask one pupil to stand next to board. Make a statement about one of the objects. T: *It's (a ball).* Pupil chooses correct object and teacher ticks board above object.

NOTE: If you want to conduct this as a formal test, go immediately to Step **1b** in Open Your Books.

OPEN YOUR BOOKS

1. Pupils open their books to page 49.
a. Play cassette. Pupils listen and point to correct picture.

1. *He's six years old.*
2. *She's seven years old.*
3. *What is it?*
   It's a big kite.
4. *What is it?*
   It's a short skipping rope.
5. *Is it a ball?*
   No, it isn't. It's a yo-yo.
6. *Is it a doll?*
   Yes, it is. It's a little doll.
7. *Can you hit a ball?*
   Yes, I can.
8. *Can you play with a yo-yo?*
   No, I can't.

b. Play cassette again. Each pupil does exercise as a written test.

2. Correct tests with pupils.

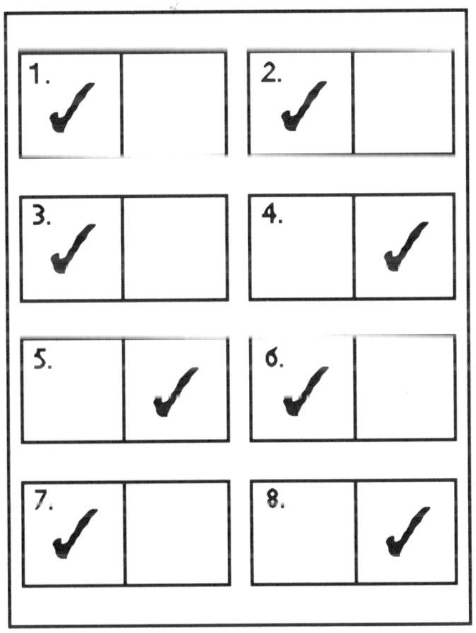

EXTENSION

1. Guessing Game (see page 6).
Teacher thinks of an object (toy or classroom object). Individual pupils try to guess what it is by asking questions. Then whole class names object in a full sentence.

P1: *Is it (big)?*
T: *(No, it isn't.)*
P2: *Is it little?*
T: *(Yes, it is.)*
P3: *Is it (a robot)?*
T: *(Yes, it is.)*
Ps: *It's a (little) (robot).*

NOTE: Colours could also be used in questions.

2. Teacher calls out a command. Pupils ask question using *Can you _______?* T: *Play with a yo-yo.* Ps: *Can you play with a yo-yo?* Teacher answers question. Pupil volunteer then calls out next command, using pictures on PB page 48 as cues, if necessary.

WORKBOOK page 52

- Pupils draw a line from each package to object inside. Then they trace names of objects and answers to first two questions. Then they write answers to last two questions. (**Answers**: *No, it is not. Yes, it is.*)
- Pupils circle correct answer to question at bottom of page (**Answer**: *a big robot*) and write this in blank. Then they practise question and answer patterns.

Unit Six

Let's Talk

LANGUAGE PATTERNS: Is the (sun) (shining)? Is the (sun) (shining) now? No, it's raining. The (sun) is (shining).

NEW VOCABULARY: sun

MATERIALS: two puppets or soft toys; tape-recorder and cassette

REVIEW

1. Sing 'The Happy Birthday Song'. Choose one pupil to be the birthday girl/boy. Pupils should point to this pupil when they sing *your*.

2. Draw six boxes on board to illustrate *big, little, long, short, round, square.* Divide class into three teams and ask each team to assign pair of adjectives correctly.

PRESENTATION

1. Present pattern.
a. Go to window and look at weather outside. (If it is not sunny, draw a simple picture of sun on board and pretend.) Use puppets to model dialogue.

Puppet A: *Is the sun shining?*
Puppet B: *Yes, it is.*
Puppet A: *Is the sun shining now?*
Puppet B: *No, it's raining.*

b. Pupils repeat each line of dialogue three times, in chorus, after each question and answer.

2. Practise.
a. Divide class into two groups and practise dialogue.

Group A: *Is the sun shining?*
Group B: *Yes, it is.*
Group A: *Is the sun shining now?*
Group B: *No, it's raining.*

Repeat so that both groups practise both parts of dialogue.

b. Draw pictures of sun and of cloud with falling rain on board. Use these to cue pupils. Divide class into pairs. Each pair of pupils should do the dialogue twice, so each pupil has a chance to practise both parts.

OPEN YOUR BOOKS

Open your Pupil's Book to page 50. Show it to pupils and ask them to name the characters. (Option: Pupils say, in own language, what they think each picture is about.)

1. Pupils open their books to page 50.
a. Play cassette. Pupils listen and point to character who is speaking.

John: *Is the sun shining?*
Lisa: *Yes, it is.*
John: *Is the sun shining now?*
Lisa: *No, it's raining.*

b. Play cassette again, stopping after each line. Pupils repeat line.

2. Present sample structures and contractions.
a. Write structures on board. Read them aloud, pointing to words. Pupils repeat.
b. Write explanation of contraction on board: *The sun is shining = The sun's shining.*
c. Pupils practise *The sun is shining* and *The sun's shining.*

3. Practise.
Divide class into two groups. Each group takes one of the roles in dialogue.

EXTENSION

1. Living Sentences (see page 7). Use the question *Is the sun shining?* Select a group of five pupils and ask them to come to front. Assign one word, in random order, to each pupil. Say the full question once. Then pupils must move so that they are standing in correct order to form question. They are not allowed to speak except to say their word. When they all think they are standing in correct order, they say sentence aloud, in chorus. Repeat with other parts of dialogue and different pupils.

2. Whispering Game (see page 7). Divide class into two groups. Ask *Is the sun shining?* Then whisper a reply to a pupil in the front of each group. (*Yes, it is* or *No, it's raining.*) That pupil whispers it to the next pupil, etc. The last pupil in each group comes to front to repeat sentence. Ask pupils to compare original sentence with final sentence to see if and how it changed.

WORKBOOK page 53

- Pupils name the characters and trace sentence in speech bubble.
- Pupils draw a line from each picture to matching sentence. Then they trace sentences.
- Pupils write an answer to question. (**Answer**: There is no one right answer—it depends on weather at time of writing.) Then they draw a picture of the weather.

Let's Sing

LANGUAGE PATTERNS: What a sunny day. Let's go out and play. Oh look!

NEW VOCABULARY: rainy, windy, sunny, snowy, day, wind

MATERIALS: two puppets or soft toys; tape-recorder and cassette; props for sunny, rainy, windy, and snowy days (e.g. sunglasses, umbrella, headscarf, woolly hat)

REVIEW

1. Use pictures on PB page 48 to cue pupils. T: *Can you (skip)?* Ps: *Yes, I can* or *No, I can't.*

2. Divide class into two groups and practise Let's Talk dialogue.

Group A: *Is the sun shining?*
Group B: *Yes, it is.*
Group A: *Is the sun shining now?*
Group B: *No, it's raining.*

PRESENTATION

1. Present new vocabulary.
a. Draw simple pictures on board to represent sunny, rainy, windy, and snowy. Point to each picture and say word. Pupils repeat each word several times.
b. Drill. Point to each picture at random and ask pupils to say word.

2. Point to each picture on board in turn and use adjective in a sentence.
a.

T: *What a sunny day!*
Pupils repeat, in chorus.

b. Repeat with rainy, windy, and snowy.

3. Practise.
Divide class into two groups to practise dialogue. Repeat so that each group practises all sentences. Use pictures on board to cue pupils.

OPEN YOUR BOOKS

Open your Pupil's Book to page 51 and show it to pupils. Ask them to name the characters and say which adjective (*sunny, windy, rainy, snowy*) they think applies to each picture.

1. Pupils open their books to page 51.
a. Play cassette. Pupils listen and point to correct picture.

The sun is shining,
the sun is shining,
What a sunny day!
The sun is shining,
the sun is shining.
Let's go out and play!

The wind is blowing,
the wind is blowing.
What a windy day!
The wind is blowing,
the wind is blowing.
Let's go out and play!

Oh look! It's raining,
Oh look! It's raining.
What a rainy day!
Oh look! It's raining,
Oh look! It's raining.
Let's go out and play!

Oh look! It's snowing,
Oh look! It's snowing.
What a snowy day!
Oh look! It's snowing,
Oh look! It's snowing.
Let's go out and play!

b. Play cassette again. Pupils sing along.

2. Practise.
Divide class into four groups: sunny, rainy, windy, and snowy. As each verse is sung, group acts out their weather (for example, holding an umbrella for rainy, building a snowman for snowy, etc.).

EXTENSION

1. Charades (see page 6). Ask for four pupil volunteers to come to front. Give each pupil a weather prop (see Materials). Pupil mimes being outside on a sunny/windy/rainy/snowy day. Class guesses type of weather and answers in a full sentence. (Ps: *The sun is shining.*) (Option: Pupils could then be asked to bring in additional props from home—different from those used.)

Let's Learn

LANGUAGE PATTERNS: How many (clouds) are there? There are six (clouds). There is one (cloud).

NEW VOCABULARY: a flower, flowers, a tree, trees, a cloud, clouds, a puddle, puddles

MATERIALS: magazine pictures (singles and multiples) of new words listed above; two puppets or soft toys; tape-recorder and cassette

REVIEW

1. Draw pictures representing the various weather types from Let's Sing on board. Pupils use picture cues to complete the dialogue. Divide class into two groups. Point to drawing of sun, for example. Group A: *The sun is shining.* Group B: *What a sunny day!* Continue with other three weather types. Then reverse roles.

2. Divide class into two groups. Assign name of toy or classroom object to each pupil in Group A and colour or adjective of size/shape to each pupil in Group B. Ask a pupil volunteer to point to one pupil from each group, at random. Each pupil says her/his word. Then class uses both words in a full sentence.

P1 (from Group A): *(Car).*
P2 (from Group B): *(Yellow).*
Ps: *It's a (yellow) (car).*
Continue with other pupils.

PRESENTATION

1. Present new vocabulary.
a. Use magazine pictures or simple board drawings to introduce new words, one pair (singular and plural) at a time. Pupils repeat each word several times.
b. Pupils practise listening to difference between singular and plural nouns. Repeat words in random order. Pupils put their hands up if they hear a plural noun.

2. Present question and answer pattern with plural nouns.
a. Draw six simple clouds on board. Use puppets to model question and answer.

Puppet A: *How many clouds are there?*
Class counts out loud with Puppet B: *One, two, three, four, five, six. There are six clouds.*

b. Pupils repeat each line of dialogue three times, in chorus.
c. Divide class into two groups. Use magazine pictures/board drawings of plural nouns (flowers, trees, clouds, puddles) to cue groups.

Group A: *How many (clouds) are there?*
Group B: *There are (three clouds).*

Groups alternate asking and answering questions.

3. Present question and answer pattern with singular nouns.
a. Show pupils magazine picture or drawing of a flower. Use puppets to model the question and answer.

Puppet A: *How many flowers are there?*
Puppet B: *There is one flower.*

b. Pupils repeat each line of dialogue three times, in chorus.
c. Show pupils magazine pictures or drawings of several flowers. Contrast difference between singular and plural.

T: *There are (three) flowers.*

Point to picture again.

T: *There is (one) flower.*

d. Pupils repeat three times, in chorus.

4. Practise.
Divide class into two groups. Use magazine pictures/board drawings to cue pupils.
Hold up or point to picture/drawing of flowers.

Group A: *How many flowers are there?*
Group B: *There are (three) flowers.*

Hold up or point to picture/drawing of clouds.

Group B: *How many clouds are there?*
Group A: *There is one cloud.*

OPEN YOUR BOOKS

Open your Pupil's Book to page 52. Show it to pupils and ask them to name the characters. Then ask them to count clouds in each picture.

1. Pupils open their books to page 52.
a. Play cassette. Pupils listen and point to clouds.

Scott: *How many clouds are there?*
John: *There are six clouds.*
Lisa: *Oh, no! There's one big cloud!*

b. Play cassette again, stopping after each line. Pupils repeat line.

2. Present sample structures and contraction.
a. Write structures on board. Read them aloud, pointing to words. Pupils repeat.
b. Write explanation of contraction on board: *There is = There's.*
c. Pupils practise *There is one cloud* and *There's one cloud.*

(Continued on page 59.)

3. Practise.

a. Divide class into two groups. Practise question and answer pattern with new vocabulary on PB page 53, using cats as models.

b. In pairs, pupils continue question and answer practice.

4. Look at activity at bottom of PB page 53.

a. In pairs, pupils look at picture of park scene. Using picture cues, pupils take turns asking and answering questions about numbers of these objects in park scene. Teacher should circulate, helping as necessary.

b. Ask individual pupils to make statements about numbers of objects in classroom (pencils, notebooks, tables, boys, girls, etc.) using *There is* and *There are.*

EXTENSION

1. Guessing Game (see page 6). Divide class into two groups. All pupils in Group A quickly draw pictures including flowers, trees, clouds, and puddles. Then each Group A pupil, in turn, tells counterpart in Group B what is in her/his picture. P1: *There is (one flower) and there are (three clouds).* Group B pupils then draw pictures following these descriptions. When they have finished, opposite pairs compare pictures and numbers.

2. Review vocabulary from Units 1, 3, 5, and 6. Divide class into two teams. Make simple board drawings of classroom objects, toys, and new words. Write numbers 1–10 on board. One pupil from each team, in turn, comes to front. T: *There are (three) (tables).* Pupil points to correct number and correct drawing and wins two points for team.

WORKBOOK pages 54 and 55

page 54

- Pupils circle correct words next to each picture. (**Answers**: *a flower, clouds, bicycles, a table.)*
- Pupils circle correct words under each picture and write them in blank. (**Answers**: *six puddles, five trees, one cloud.*) They can then practise question and answer pattern.

page 55

- Pupils trace words. Then they write a sentence to describe each picture. (**Answers**: *It's raining. It's snowing. It's windy.* or *The wind is blowing.*)
- Pupils trace words. Then they write a sentence about numbers of objects in each picture. (**Answers**: *There are three balls. There are two rackets. There is one bicycle. There is one flower. There are two cats.*)

Let's Learn Some More

LANGUAGE PATTERNS: Where is my ball? It is in/on/under/by the bag. Where is it? Where are they?

NEW VOCABULARY: in, on, under, by

MATERIALS: two puppets or soft toys; small ball and school bag; tape-recorder and cassette

REVIEW

1. Draw single and multiple objects for Units 1, 3, and 6 vocabulary on board. Point to each drawing (in random order) and ask individual pupils to count and name objects. P1: *There are (three) (clouds)* or *There is (one) (cloud).*

2. Divide class into two teams. Two pupils, one from each team, come to board. P1 from Team A points to a drawing and asks P1 from Team B: *How many _______ are there?* P1 from Team B answers the question using *There is* or *There are.* Correct questions and answers earn one point. Then another pupil from Team A comes to the front and P1 from Team B asks a question.

PRESENTATION

1. Present new vocabulary.
a. Place a bag where all pupils can see it. Put a small ball on top of bag and say: *on.* Pupils repeat several times. Continue with *under, by,* and *in.* After introducing each new preposition, conduct a quick mini-drill, alternating new word with previously introduced words.
b. Put ball on, under, by, and in bag respectively. Pupils say correct preposition.

2. Present pattern.
a. Use bag and ball as in **1**. Use puppets to model question and answer.

Puppet A: *Where is the ball?*
Puppet B: *The ball is on the bag.*

b. Pupils repeat each line of dialogue three times, in chorus. As pupils repeat, teacher should point to ball and bag in turn.
c. Repeat Steps **a** and **b** for *under, by,* and *in.*

3. Practise.
a. Silent drill. Assign each preposition *(in, on, under, by)* to a different pupil or group of pupils. Use ball and bag. Place ball in bag. The pupil(s) who was/were assigned *in* should stand up and then sit down. It is not necessary for teacher or pupil(s) to speak. Continue with other prepositions.
b. Divide class into two groups. Use ball and bag to cue groups.

T: (Shows ball under bag.)
Group A: *Where is the ball?*
Group B: *The ball is under the bag.*

Groups alternate asking and answering questions.
c. In pairs, (one pair at a time) pupils practise asking and answering questions. Teacher puts classroom objects in different locations around classroom (in/on/under/by the desk/notebook/bag/pencil case, etc.). P1: *Where is the (notebook)?* P2: *The (notebook) is on the desk.*

4. Introduce *it* and *they.* Hold up a pencil and then place it on table. T: *Where is the pencil?* Pupils answer: *The pencil is on the table.* T: *Where is it?* Pupils answer: *It is on the table.* Put two pencils on table. T: *Where are the pencils?* Pupils answer. T: *Where are they?* Pupils answer. Drill, using one and two pencils to cue pupils.

OPEN YOUR BOOKS

Open your Pupil's Book to page 54. Show it to pupils and ask them to name the characters. (Option: Pupils say, in own language, what they think each picture is about.)

1. Pupils open their books to page 54.
a. Play cassette. Pupils listen and point to character who is speaking.

Lisa: *Where's the kite?*
Scott: *It's in the tree.*
John: *Where are the books?*
Lisa: *They're under the table.*

b. Play cassette again, stopping after each line. Pupils repeat line.

2. Present sample structures and contractions.
a. Write structures on board. Read them aloud, pointing to words. Pupils repeat.
b. Write explanation of contractions on board:
Where is = Where's
It is = It's
They are = They're

c. Pupils practise *Where is my ball?, Where's my ball?, It is in the bag, It's in the bag, They are under the table,* and *They're under the table.*

3. Practise.
Look at activity at top of PB page 55.
a. Model questions presented by cats. Pupils repeat.
b. Divide class into two groups. Each group practises asking and answering questions using picture cues.

T: *Doll.*
Group A: *Where is it?*
Group B: *It's under the table.*
T: *Balls.*
Group B: *Where are they?*
Group A: *They're in the bag.*

c. In pairs, pupils practise asking and answering questions, using picture cues. Teacher should circulate, helping pupils as necessary.

(Continued on page 61.)

EXTENSION

1. Picture Dictation (see page 7). Pupil volunteers tell class what to draw, using prepositions and numbers. Example: *There are five flowers in the puddle,* etc.

2. Give instructions to class about location of classroom objects. Hold up a pen. Ps: *Where is the pen?* T: *It's under the book.* Pupils put pens under books.

WORKBOOK pages 56 and 57

page 56

- Pupils circle correct preposition next to each object. (**Answers**: *on, in, under, by.*) Then they trace prepositions.
- Pupils circle correct preposition next to each picture. (**Answers**: *in, by, under, in.*) Then they write prepositions in blanks under pictures. Pupils can then practise question and answer pattern.

page 57

- Pupils trace words. Then they write answer to each question, using information in picture. (**Answers**: *Yes, it is. / No, it isn't. It's a tree. / Yes, it is.*)
- Pupils circle correct word next to each sentence. (**Answers**: *No, Yes, Yes, Yes, No, Yes.*)
- Pupils colour picture as instructed.

Let's Learn the Alphabet

NEW VOCABULARY: octopus, question

MATERIALS: tape-recorder and cassette; lined paper

1. Review letters *A–N*. Assign a letter *A–N* to each pupil. All pupils recite alphabet from A to N. As each pupil's letter is called, pupil must stand up.

2. Pupils open their books to bottom of page 55.

a. Play cassette. Pupils listen and point to letters.

Teacher: *O, octopus; P, pencil; Q, question; R, ruler.*

b. Play cassette again, stopping after each letter. Pupils repeat letter and word.

c. Say word *octopus* carefully, emphasizing initial sound. Print word *octopus* on board and underline *o*.

d. Print letter *o* next to word *octopus* on board.

o—octopus

Ask pupils to think of other words that begin with the same sound (e.g. *orange*).

e. Repeat Steps **c** and **d** for words *pencil, question,* and *ruler.*

3. Show pupils how to print a small *o*. Then introduce capital *O*. Repeat for letters *P, Q,* and *R*. Practise printing letters on lined paper.

WORKBOOK page 58

- Pupils write correct letter (small) to complete each word.
- Pupils circle initial letter of word that appears under each box. Then they trace words.

Let's Move

LANGUAGE PATTERNS: I'm (climbing a tree)/(playing tennis). He's (reading a book)/(flying a kite). She's (playing tag) (riding a bicycle). Is he (climbing a tree)?

NEW VOCABULARY: climbing, riding, flying, reading, tag, tennis, tree

MATERIALS: single and multiple classroom objects; tape-recorder and cassette

REVIEW

1. Chain Drill (see page 6). Use six activity pictures on page 48 to cue pupils. P1 asks: *Can you (play with a yo-yo)?* P2 answers: *Yes, I can* or *No, I can't.*

2. Review prepositions using classroom objects. Divide class into two groups. Arrange single and multiple objects in various locations around classroom. Point to object(s). Group A asks: *Where is it/are they?* Group B answers: *(It's) (on) (the table).* Reverse roles for next object(s).

PRESENTATION

1. Present action sentences.
a. (**NOTE**: For clarity, use first person *I'm* to present the verbs, although other pronouns are used in Pupil's Book.) Model sentences using clear gestures. For *I'm riding a bicycle* and *I'm climbing a tree*, teacher can draw bicycle and tree on board, and then do riding and climbing actions.
b. Say sentences. Pupils listen and mime actions.
c. Repeat sentences, stopping after each one. Pupils listen, repeat, and mime action.
d. Divide class into two groups and practise sentences. Groups take turns giving and acting out sentences. Draw objects on board (tree, tennis racket, book, child running, bicycle, kite) to cue pupils.

OPEN YOUR BOOKS

Open your Pupil's Book to page 56 and show it to pupils. Point to each picture in turn and say sentence. Pupils repeat sentence and mime action.

1. Pupils open their books to page 56.
a. Play cassette, stopping after *He's flying a kite.* Pupils listen and point to each action.

I'm climbing a tree.
I'm playing tennis.
He's reading a book.
She's playing tag.
She's riding a bicycle.
He's flying a kite.

b. Play cassette again, stopping after each sentence. Pupils repeat sentence.

2. Say sentences in random order. Pupils point to correct picture and repeat sentence.

3. Ask pupils, one at a time, to point to a picture and say sentence (with teacher's help). Class repeats sentence and mimes action.

4. Present sample structures and contraction.
a. Write structures on board. Read them aloud, pointing to words. Pupils repeat.
b. Write explanation of contraction on board: *is not = isn't.*
c. Play rest of cassette for this page. Pupils listen and point to pictures at bottom of page 56.

Is he climbing a tree?
Yes, he is.
No, he isn't!

d. Play cassette again, stopping after each line. Pupils repeat line.

4. Practise.
Use drawings made for **1d**. Cross out three of them. T: (to class) *Is she playing tennis?* (Points to drawing that has not been crossed out.) Ps: *Yes, she is.* If drawing has been crossed out pupils answer: *No, (she) isn't.*

EXTENSION

1. Use drawings made of objects for **1d** but don't cross any out. Ask a boy and a girl to stand beside board. Point to an object and to either a girl or boy as you ask each pupil in turn: *Is (Ann) (reading a book)?* etc. Pupil answers: *Yes, (she) is* or *No, (she) isn't.*

WORKBOOK page 59

- Pupils trace words in sentence above each picture. Then they circle correct answer. (**Answers**: *Yes, he is. No, she isn't. No, he isn't. Yes, she is. Yes, he is. No, she isn't.*)

Let's Listen

LANGUAGE PATTERNS: Unit review

VOCABULARY: Unit review

MATERIALS: two teacher-made cards with *is* and *isn't* written on them; classroom objects; tape-recorder and cassette

REVIEW

1. Let's Talk.
Divide class into two groups and sing 'Let's Go Out and Play' alternating verses between groups.

2. Let's Learn.
Divide class into two teams. Whisper a different sentence to first pupil in each team. T: *There are (six) (clouds).* Pupils whisper the sentences to each other until they reach last pupil in team. This pupil draws appropriate number of objects on board. Award points for drawing correct number and correct objects.

3. Let's Learn Some More.
Place familiar objects around classroom in places that pupils can describe. T: *Where's (the yellow pencil)?* Ps: *(It's) (under) (the desk).*

4. Let's Move.
Draw tree, tennis racket, book, bicycle and kite on board. Put two teacher-made cards with *is* and *isn't* on them on board rail. Ask a boy and a girl to stand by board. Then ask another pupil to come forward. Pupil points to girl or boy, chooses a card and holds it up, and points to a drawing. Class must make an appropriate statement about pupil + card + drawing—e.g. *(She) (isn't) (riding a bicycle).*

PRESENTATION

Teach pupils how to do test. Draw single and multiple flower(s), tree(s), cloud(s), and puddle(s) on board. Ask one pupil to stand next to board. Make a statement about one of the drawings.

T: *It's (a flower).*

Pupil points to correct drawing and teacher ticks board above drawing.

NOTE: If you want to conduct this as a formal test, go immediately to Step **1b** in Open Your Books.

OPEN YOUR BOOKS

1. Pupils open their books to page 57.
a. Play cassette. Pupils listen and point to correct picture.

1. *Is the sun shining?*
   Yes, it is.
2. *Is it snowing?*
   No, it isn't.
3. *Where's the kite?*
   It's under the tree.
4. *Where's the book?*
   It's on the table.
5. *How many puddles are there?*
   There are four puddles.
6. *How many flowers are there?*
   There's one flower.
7. *Can he fly a kite?*
   Yes, he can.
8. *Can she ride a bicycle?*
   No, she can't.

b. Play cassette again. Each pupil does exercise as a written test.

2. Correct tests with pupils.

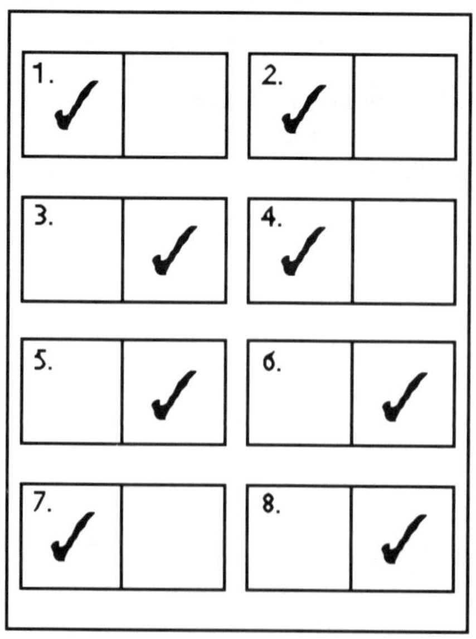

EXTENSION

1. Picture Dictation (see page 7).
One pupil volunteer tells class what to draw on board or on a piece of paper. P: *Draw a tree. Draw eight kites in the tree.* Pupils can use previous vocabulary, for example, *Draw a long pencil by the table,* etc.

2. Using commands stand, sit, put, go, and draw, give pupils instructions involving prepositions. T: *Stand by the table. Sit on the chair. Put the short pencil in the bag. Go to the board and draw two flowers under one cloud.*

3. Spot the Changes. Place three or four objects in, on, under, or by others and say where each is. T: *The (pencil) is (under) (the table).* Then ask a pupil to go out of the room or face the other way while another pupil rearranges objects. On returning, P1 must spot the new locations and describe them.

WORKBOOK page 60

- Pupils circle correct sentence next to each picture. (**Answers**: *It is windy, It is snowing.*) Then they say sentences.
- Pupils trace preposition in each sentence. Then they draw objects in correct positions around table.
- Pupils trace words. Then they complete each sentence by writing a number in blank. (**Answers**: *two, one.*) Then they practise question and answer pattern.

Let's Review

SENTENCE PATTERNS: General review

VOCABULARY: General review

MATERIALS: bag or box filled with toys; tape-recorder, music cassette, and *Let's Speak English* cassette; sets of dice; two small bags for toy drawings

REVIEW

1. Songs.

a. Sing 'The Happy Birthday Song' and 'Let's Go Out and Play' as a whole class.

b. One pupil does actions to indicate a certain type of weather (for example, making a noise like wind). Class must guess what type of weather is being demonstrated. Ps: *It's a windy day!* Continue until all pupils have acted out a type of weather.

c. Draw a yo-yo, kite, toy car, ball, doll, puzzle, robot, skipping rope, tennis racket, and bicycle on board. One pupil comes up to board and points to a drawing and to another pupil.

P1: *Happy Birthday, (Amy). This is for you.*
P2: *(A yo-yo)! Thank you.*

Continue for one or two minutes with different pupils.

2. Vocabulary.

a. Pupils form a circle or remain seated. Fill a bag with various shapes and sizes of toys (see PB page 45). As pupils pass bag around, play some music. When music stops, pupil holding bag pulls out one toy and identifies it, using an adjective. P1: *(A round ball.)* Continue until each pupil has identified one toy.

b. Use a desk and a book to quickly review prepositions *(in, on, under, by)*. Move book around desk and ask class to say where it is.

3. Structures.

a. Guessing Game (see page 6). One pupil opens book to page 45, decides on an object, and describes it. Class then guesses what it is.

P1: *It's (round).*
P2: *Is it (a yo-yo)?*
P1: *No, it isn't.*
P3: *Is it (a ball)?*
P1: *Yes, it is.*

Continue with a few more objects and different leaders.

b. In pairs, pupils ask each other how many of various items are in their bookbags. P1: *How many (pencils) are there?* P2: *There are (three) (pencils).* Teacher should circulate, helping pupils as necessary.

c. Divide class into two groups. Use realia to practise prepositions in statements. Place one or more items in, on, under, or by an object in classroom. Group A asks *Where is it?* or *Where are they?* Group B answers *It's (by the door). They're (under the chair).*

OPEN YOUR BOOKS

1. Say these.
Pupils open their books to page 58. Teacher circulates as pupils do the following activities.

a. Pupils review vocabulary by pointing to each picture in order and calling out name of picture, in chorus. (**Answers**: *a big flower, a little flower, a long skipping rope, a short skipping rope, a round box, a square box, a big bicycle, a little bicycle, a big tree, a little tree.*)

b. Divide class into pairs. Give each pair a dice. Pupils take turns rolling dice, moving number of spaces equal to number on dice and identifying picture. Pupils continue game until one pupil lands directly on goal.

c. Divide class into pairs. P1 identifies all picture cues as quickly as possible. P2 listens and helps P1 if necessary. If all pictures are identified correctly, P1 receives 10 points. Reverse roles and play again.

2. Answer the question.
Divide class into two groups. Group A asks Group B the following. Group A: *How many (dolls) are there?* Group B: *There are (three) (dolls).* Continue for each item in picture, reversing roles.

3. Say and act.

a. Look at pictures at bottom of page 58. Point to speech bubble in first picture and say *How old are you?* Point to blank speech bubble and ask pupils to guess what should be there. (**Answer**: *I'm (seven) years old.*) Repeat for second picture. (**Answer**: *Is the sun shining?*)

b. In pairs, pupils practise both dialogues. Teacher should circulate, helping as necessary.

(Continued on page 66.)

4. Ask your partner.
In pairs, pupils interview each other using picture cues on questionnaire. P1: *Can you (climb a tree)?* P2: *Yes, I can* or *No, I can't.* Pupils should tick either *Yes* or *No* after each question to match their partner's answers. Each pupil asks and answers questions. Teacher should circulate, helping pupils as necessary.

5. Listen carefully.

a. Play cassette. Pupils listen and point to correct picture.

a: *The cat is under the tree.*
b: *The cat is in the box.*
c: *The cat is on the table.*
d: *The cat is by the bag.*

b. Play cassette again. Pupils listen and tick small box next to correct answer.

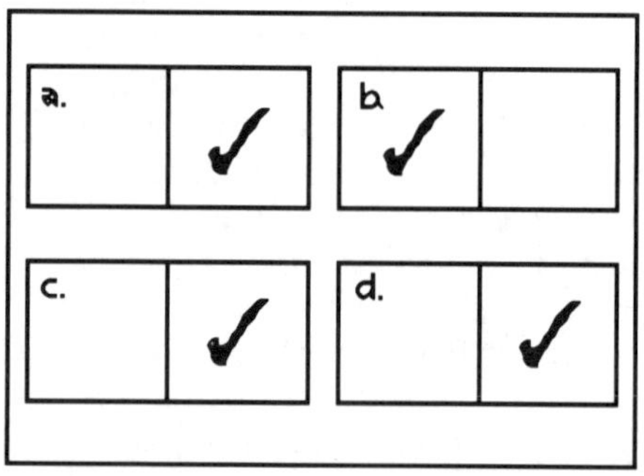

c. Pupils identify the other four pictures and say sentences. (*The cat is in the tree. The cat is on the box. The cat is by the table. The cat is in the bag.*) Then they say all eight sentences.

EXTENSION

1. Birthday Party. All pupils draw a toy on a piece of paper. They fold their papers and put them in bag. One pupil at a time is the birthday child. Class says *Happy birthday, (Sue). This is for you.* P1 pulls a paper out of bag, looks at it and says *Wow! A (bicycle)! Thank you!* Continue until all pupils have received a birthday gift.

WORKBOOK pages 61 and 62

page 61
- Pupils write first letter of each word in blank. Then they trace words.
- Pupils find and circle words in box.

page 62
- Pupils draw a line from each cat to adjective that describes it. Then they trace adjectives.
- Pupils draw a line from each object to the sentence that describes its position in picture above. Then they trace prepositions.

Unit Seven

Let's Talk

LANGUAGE PATTERNS: I'm (hungry). I want (an apple). I want (some juice). Here you are. Thank you. You're welcome.

NEW VOCABULARY: hungry, thirsty, juice, you're welcome

MATERIALS: carton or bottle of fruit juice; apple; two puppets or soft toys; tape-recorder and cassette

REVIEW

1. Sing 'Lets Go Out and Play'. Class sings it once together for review. Then divide class into five groups representing sunny, cloudy, rainy, windy, and snowy. Sing the song again, each group standing to sing their verse.

2. Demonstrate prepositions *(by, on, in,* and *under)* by moving two objects familiar to pupils (a notebook and a pencil, for example) into various positions. T: *Where is it?* (Pointing to pencil.) Ps: *It's on the notebook.*

PRESENTATION

1. Present new vocabulary.
a. Place carton or bottle of juice on table. T: *Juice, juice.* Ps: *Juice.*
b. Use actions to demonstrate *thirsty.* Say word and ask pupils to repeat.
c. Repeat **b** for *hungry,* using an apple.

2. Present first part of dialogue.
a. Use puppets to model pattern. Place apple on table. Puppet A looks at apple. Puppet A: *I'm hungry. I want an apple.*
b. Pupils repeat three times, in chorus.
c. Place carton or bottle of juice on table and repeat Steps **a** and **b** for *I'm thirsty. I want some juice.*

3. Present second part of dialogue.
a. Use puppets to model second part of dialogue. Puppet B picks up apple and hands it to Puppet A (or moves it towards Puppet A).

Puppet B: *Here you are.*
Puppet A: *Thank you.*
Puppet B: *You're welcome.*

b. Pupils repeat each line of dialogue three times, in chorus.

4. Practise.
a. Divide class into two groups.

Group A: *I'm hungry. I want an apple.*
Group B: *Here you are.*
Group A: *Thank you.*
Group B: *You're welcome.*

Group B: *I'm thirsty. I want some juice.*
Group A: *Here you are.*
Group B: *Thank you.*
Group A: *You're welcome.*

b. Pupils practise dialogue in pairs, miming giving, eating, and drinking.

P1: *I'm thirsty. I want some juice.*
P2: *Here you are.*
P1: *Thank you.*
P2: *You're welcome.*

Teacher should circulate to make sure pupils are using *thirsty* with the object *juice* and *hungry* with *apple.*

OPEN YOUR BOOKS

Open your Pupil's Book to page 60 and show it to pupils. Ask them to name the characters and say what they think characters are saying.

1. Pupils open their books to page 60.
a. Play cassette. Pupils listen and point to character who is speaking.

Lisa: *I'm hungry. I want an apple.*
Jenny: *I'm thirsty. I want some juice.*
Lisa: *Here you are.*
Jenny: *Thank you.*
Lisa: *You're welcome.*

b. Play cassette again, stopping after each line. Pupils repeat line.

2. Present sample structures and contraction.
a. Write structures on board. Read them aloud, pointing to words. Pupils repeat.
b. Put explanation of contraction on board: *You are = You're.*
c. Pupils practise *You are welcome* and *You're welcome.*

3. Practise.
a. Divide class into two groups and practise dialogue.
b. In pairs, pupils continue to practise dialogue.

EXTENSION

1. Ask pupils, in turn, to find a classroom object.

T: *I want (a pencil).*
P1: *Here you are.* (Holds pencil up.)
T: *Thank you.*
P1: *You're welcome.*

WORKBOOK page 63

- Pupils trace words next to pictures.
- Pupils trace adjectives. Then they complete sentences by writing names of objects shown in thought bubbles. (**Answers**: *an apple, some juice.*) Then they say sentences.
- Pupils trace sentence. Then they say dialogue.

Let's Sing

LANGUAGE PATTERNS: What do you want?

NEW VOCABULARY: peaches, plums

MATERIALS: single and multiple classroom objects; two peaches, two apples, two plums (or magazine pictures of these); two puppets or soft toys; tape-recorder and cassette

REVIEW

1. Living Dialogues (see page 7). On five separate pieces of paper write lines of dialogue from Unit 7 Let's Talk. (*I'm hungry. I want an apple. Here you are. Thank you. You're welcome.*) Give these to five pupils (or duplicate so that two or more pupils have same line). Start dialogue by drawing apple on board. Pupil with first line of dialogue comes to front and says it. P1: *I'm hungry.* Then pupil with next line comes up and stands next to P1. P2: *I want an apple.* When all five lines are complete the five pupils say them, quickly, one line after another, and class repeats.

2. Drill. Use single and multiple classroom objects and board drawings of toys (see PB page 45) as cues. Hold up object or point to drawing. Ps: *I want (a pen)* or *I want (some pens).*

PRESENTATION

1. Present new vocabulary.
a. Show pupils a peach (or picture of peach). Put it on the table. T: *Peach.* Put another peach next to it. T: *Peaches.* Pupils repeat.
b. Repeat Step **a** for apples and plums.

2. Present pattern.
a. Use puppets to model question and answer.

Puppet A: *What do you want?*
Puppet B: *I want an apple.*

Puppet A gives apple to Puppet B, if possible, or touches apple. Pupils repeat each line of dialogue three times, in chorus.
b. Repeat question and answer for *peaches* and *plums.*

NOTE: Explain to pupils that we use *some* with plural nouns.

3. Practise.
a. Divide class in half and chant the song. Clap to keep rhythm.

Whole Class: *Peaches, apples, and plums,*
Peaches, apples, and plums.
Group A: *What do you want?*
Group B: *I want an apple.*
Whole Class: *Peaches, apples, and plums.*

b. Repeat several times, alternating Groups A and B. Each time, teacher can cue Group B by holding up apple(s), peach(es), or plum(s) or pictures of these. Pupils should ask for that fruit, using *some* with plurals.

OPEN YOUR BOOKS

Open your Pupil's Book to page 61. Show it to pupils and ask them to name the fruits. (**Answers**: *bananas, orange, apple, plums, peach, pear, grapes, strawberries.*)

1. Pupils open their books to page 61.
a. Play cassette. Pupils listen and point to correct fruit.

Peaches, apples, and plums,
Peaches, apples, and plums.
What do you want?
I want an apple.
Peaches, apples, and plums.
Repeat.

b. Play cassette again. Pupils sing along.

2. Practise.
Play cassette. Then divide class into two groups. All pupils sing *Peaches, apples, and plums,* Group A sings *What do you want?,* and Group B sings *I want an apple.*

EXTENSION

1. Divide class into pairs. Pupils use classroom objects or pictures on PB page 45 as cues. One pair at a time practises dialogue.
P1: *What do you want?*
P2: *I want (a book).*
P1: *Here you are.* (Presents object or points to picture.)
P2: *Thank you.*
P1: *You're welcome.*

2. Memory Chain (see page 7). Divide class into two or three teams. In turn, each team tries to make chain as long as possible without forgetting any items. Each pupil in team adds one item to chain of lines.
P1: *I like (apples).*
P2: *I like (apples) and (melons).*
P3: *I like (apples) and (melons) and (oranges).*

3. The Fruit Song.
a. Bring in other kinds of seasonal fruit and teach their English names to the pupils: T: *A lemon.* Ps: *A lemon, a lemon.*
b. Sing 'Peaches, Apples, and Plums' again without cassette, substituting the names of other fruits. Pupil volunteers can sing solo lines and 'choose' the fruit they want.

All: *(Oranges), (lemons), and (pears).*
(Repeat.)
P1: *What do you want?*
P2: *I want (an orange).*
All: *(Oranges), (lemons), and (pears).*

Let's Learn

LANGUAGE PATTERNS: I want (some cake) and (some ice cream).

NEW VOCABULARY: cake, ice cream, milk, chicken, fish, pizza, rice, bread

MATERIALS: magazine pictures of new words listed above; two puppets or soft toys; tape-recorder and cassette; beanbag or ball

REVIEW

1. Sing 'Peaches, Apples, and Plums'. Divide class into three groups. One group stands when they sing *peaches,* the second stands when they sing *apples,* and the third stands when they sing *plums.* The whole class sits as they sing *What do you want? I want an apple.*

2. Choose vocabulary to review from Units 1–6 and draw single and multiple pictures on board. Two pupil volunteers come up to board and each points to a picture. Ps: *I want (an apple) and (some pencils).*

PRESENTATION

1. Present new vocabulary.
a. Use magazine pictures or simple board drawings to introduce new vocabulary words, one at a time. Point to each picture and say word. Pupils repeat several times. After introducing each new word, conduct a quick mini-drill, alternating new word with previously introduced words.
b. Drill. Point to each picture at random and ask individual pupils to say word.

2. Present question and answer pattern.
a. Put magazine pictures of cake and ice cream on board rail or use board drawings. Use puppets to model question and answer.

Puppet A: *What do you want?*
Puppet B: *I want some cake.* (Touches picture.)

Pupils repeat each line of dialogue three times, in chorus.
NOTE: Explain to pupils that we use *some* with uncountable nouns.

b. Repeat with picture of ice cream, reversing roles.

Puppet B: *What do you want?*
Puppet A: *I want some ice cream.* (Touches picture.)

Pupils repeat each line of dialogue three times.
c. Make Puppet B touch both cake and ice cream pictures and model the final pattern.

Puppet B: *Oh! I want some cake and some ice cream.*

Pupils repeat three times, in chorus.

3. Practise.
a. Divide class into two groups. Use magazine pictures or simple board drawings of new words to cue groups.

Group A: *What do you want?*
(Teacher touches pictures of chicken and rice.)
Group B: *I want (some chicken) and (some rice).*

Groups should alternate asking and answering questions.
b. Chain Drill (see page 6). Use magazine pictures or board drawings to cue pupils.

P1 to P2: *What do you want?*
P2: *I want (some chicken) and (some rice).*
P2 to p3: *What do you want?*

OPEN YOUR BOOKS

Open your Pupil's Book to page 62 and show it to pupils. Ask them to name the characters and say what they think characters are saying.

1. Pupils open their books to page 62.
a. Play cassette. Pupils listen and point to character who is speaking.

Andy: *I'm hungry.*
Kate: *What do you want?*
Andy: *I want some cake. What do you want?*
Kate: *I want some ice cream.*
Andy: *Oh! I want some cake and some ice cream.*

b. Play cassette again, stopping after each line. Pupils repeat line.

2. Present sample structures.
a. Write structures on board. Read them aloud, pointing to words. Pupils repeat.
b. Pupils practise structures in two groups. Draw cake and ice cream on board as cues.

3. Practise.
a. Divide class into two groups. Practise question and answer pattern with new vocabulary on PB page 63, using two cats as models.
b. Pupils continue question and answer practice in pairs.

4. Look at activity at bottom of page 63.
a. Teacher points to each picture in turn.

T: *What do you want?*
Ps: *I want (some rice) and (some chicken).*

b. In turn, each pupil says a sentence about any two items of food shown on page 63. P1: *I want (some bread) and (some chicken).*

(Continued on page 70.)

EXTENSION

1. **Bingo** (see page 6). Pupils draw food items on grid.

WORKBOOK pages 64 and 65

page 64

- Pupils trace food labels below pictures.
- Pupils complete sentence with names of two food items of their choice. Then they draw these two items in box.

page 65

- Pupils trace words. Then they write sentences using present continuous. (**Answers**: *He's flying a kite. She's riding a bicycle. I'm playing tennis. He's reading a book.*)
- Pupils complete dialogue, using information from picture of Jenny and John. (**Answers**: John: *I'm hungry. I want a peach.* / Jenny: *I'm thirsty. I want some juice.* / John: *Here you are.* / Jenny: *Thank you.*/ John: *You're welcome.*)
- Pupils write two sentences for each picture. (**Answers:** *I'm thirsty. I want some milk.* or *I want some juice.* / *I'm hungry. I want some chicken.*)

Let's Learn Some More

LANGUAGE PATTERNS: Do you want (some chicken)? Yes, I do. No, I don't.

VOCABULARY: Unit review

MATERIALS: two puppets or soft toys; tape-recorder and cassette; slips of paper, enough for whole class, with ticks or crosses on them (half each)

REVIEW

1. On board draw pictures of food from Let's Learn, as well as any earlier vocabulary you want to review. Teacher says *I want (some pizza) and (some fish)* and points to a pupil. Pupil must come up and indicate correct drawings.

2. Point to a drawing of food/drink. Pupils must say either *I'm hungry. I want (some pizza)* or *I'm thirsty. I want (some milk)* depending on drawing indicated.

PRESENTATION

1. Present first pattern.
a. Use puppets to model first question and answer.

Puppet A: (Pointing to drawing of chicken.) *Do you want some chicken?*
Puppet B: *Yes, I do.*

b. Pupils repeat each line of dialogue three times, in chorus.

2. Practise.
a. Divide class into two groups. Point to board drawings to cue groups.

Group A: *Do you want some chicken?*
Group B: *Yes, I do.*

Groups alternate asking and answering questions.
b. Chain Drill (see page 6). Pupils use pictures on PB page 63 as cues.

P1: *Do you want (some chicken)?*
P2: *Yes, I do. Do you want (some pizza)?*
P3: *Yes, I do. Do you want (some rice)?*

3. Present second pattern.
a. Use puppets to model second question and negative answer.

Puppet B: (Pointing to drawing of chicken.) *Do you want some chicken?*
Puppet A: *No, I don't. I want some pizza.*

b. Pupils repeat each line of dialogue three times, in chorus.

4. Practise.
a. Chain Drill (see page 6). Point to board drawings to cue pupils.

P1: *Do you want (some chicken)?*
P2: *No, I don't. I want (some pizza). Do you want (some pizza)?*
P3: *No, I don't. I want (some ice cream). Do you want (some ice cream)?*

b. Pupils practise asking and answering questions in pairs, using pictures on page 63. They should vary their answers, using both *Yes, I do* and *No, I don't.*

OPEN YOUR BOOKS

Open your Pupil's Book to page 64 and show it to pupils. Ask them to name the characters.

1. Pupils open their books to page 64.
a. Play cassette. Pupils listen and point to character who is speaking.

Scott: *Do you want some chicken?*
John: *Yes, I do. Do you want some chicken?*
Scott: *No, I don't. I want some pizza.*

b. Play cassette again, stopping after each line. Pupils repeat line.

2. Present sample structures.
a. Write structures on board. Read them aloud, pointing to words. Pupils repeat.
b. Write explanation of contraction on board: *do not = don't.*
c. Pupils practise *No, I don't* and *No, I do not.*

3. Practise.
Look at activity at top of PB page 65.
a. Divide class into two groups. Each group alternates asking and answering questions using picture cues and following model given by cats.
b. Pupils continue question and answer practice in pairs.

EXTENSION

1. Divide class into two groups. Hand out slips of paper with ticks and crosses on them to Group B. Pupils in Group A alternate asking questions to pupils in Group B, using pictures of food on page 65. P1 (from Group A): *Do you want (some bread)?* P1 from Group B answers *Yes, I do* or *No, I don't,* depending on whether her/his paper has tick or cross on it.

2. Draw simple pictures of chicken, fish, pizza, rice, bread, milk, cake, and ice cream on board. Two or more pupils come up to board together and each asks question, in turn, naming a different food item.

P1: *Do you want (some chicken)?*
T: *No, I don't.*
P2: *Do you want (some ice cream)?*
T: *Yes, I do.*

When teacher answers *Yes, I do,* pupil who has asked question points to picture and pretends to give food item to teacher.

P: *Here you are.*
T: *Thank you.*
P: *You're welcome.*

(Continued on page 72.)

WORKBOOK pages 66 and 67

page 66

- Pupils trace answers to questions.
- Pupils circle answer of their choice next to each picture. Then they write answer under picture. Then they practise question and answer pattern.

page 67

- Pupils trace sample questions and answers. Then they write questions and answers about pairs of pictures. (**Answers**: *Do you want some juice? Yes, I do. / Do you want some rice? No, I don't. I want some bread. / Do you want some pizza? Yes, I do.*)
- Pupils trace sample sentence. Then they rewrite remaining sentences, using full forms. (**Answers**: *There is one cloud. I am hungry. You are welcome. Where is the kite? I am reading a book. They are under the table.*)

Let's Learn the Alphabet

NEW VOCABULARY: umbrella, van

MATERIALS: tape-recorder and cassette; lined paper

1. Review letters *A–R*. Assign a letter *A–R* to each pupil. All pupils recite alphabet from A to R. As each pupil's letter is called, that pupil must stand up.

2. Pupils open their books to bottom of page 65.

a. Play cassette. Pupils listen and point to letters.

Teacher: *S, sun; T, table; U, umbrella; V, van.*

b. Play cassette again, stopping after each letter. Pupils say letter and word.

c. Say word *sun* carefully, emphasizing initial sound. Print word *sun* on board and underline *s*.

d. Print *s* next to word *sun* on board.

s—sun

Ask pupils to think of other words that begin with the same sound (e.g. *seven*).

c. Repeat Steps **c** and **d** for words *table, umbrella,* and *van.*

3. Show pupils how to print a small *s*. Then introduce capital *S*. Repeat for letters *T, U,* and *V*. Practise printing letters on lined paper.

WORKBOOK page 68

- Pupils draw a line from each set of letters to picture whose name begins with that letter and then to name itself. Then they trace names.
- Pupils circle letter which is the same as first letter of word under picture. Then they trace words.

Let's Move

LANGUAGE PATTERNS: I'm buying (an apple). I'm washing/cutting/eating it. I'm buying some juice. I'm opening/pouring/drinking it.

NEW VOCABULARY: buying, washing, cutting, pouring, drinking

MATERIALS: coins; apple; carton or bottle of juice; glass; tape-recorder and cassette

REVIEW

1. Charades (see page 6). Whisper commands from PB page 48 and phrases from page 56 to cue pupils.

2. Divide class into two groups. Group A represents sentence *I want an apple;* Group B represents sentence *I want some juice.*

T: *I'm hungry.*
Group A: (stands) *I want an apple.*
T: *I'm thirsty.*
Group B: (stands) *I want some juice.*

PRESENTATION

1. Present sentences.
a. Model sentences using clear gestures. Using coins and an apple, mime buying the apple. T: *I'm buying an apple.* Mime washing apple. T: *I'm washing it.* Cut it in half or in quarters. T: *I'm cutting it.* Take a bite out of it. T: *I'm eating it.*
b. Say sentences. Pupils listen and mime actions.
c. Repeat sentences, stopping after each one. Pupils listen, repeat, and mime action.
d. Repeat Steps **a**, **b**, and **c** for *juice* sequence.
e. Divide class into two groups and play **Charades.** Whisper sentences to cue pupils.

OPEN YOUR BOOKS

Open your Pupil's Book to page 66 and show it to pupils. Point to each picture in turn and say sentence. Pupils repeat sentence and mime action.

1. Pupils open their books to page 66.
a. Play cassette. Pupils listen and point to each action.

I'm buying an apple.
I'm washing it.
I'm cutting it.
I'm eating it.
I'm buying some juice.
I'm opening it.
I'm pouring it.
I'm drinking it.

b. Play cassette again, stopping after each sentence. Pupils repeat sentence.

2. Say sentences in random order. Pupils point to correct pictures and repeat sentences.

3. Ask pupils, one at a time, to point to a picture and say sentence (with teacher's help). Class repeats sentence and mimes action.

4. Pupils look at pictures on bottom of page 66.
a. Divide class into two groups and alternate asking and answering questions using picture cues. Group A: *Can you (eat) it?* Group B: *Yes* or *No.*
b. Repeat, using picture cues on PB page 63.

5. Practise.
a. Divide class into two groups. Draw simple food pictures on board and print *eat* and *drink.* Point to a food drawing to cue groups. Teacher points to milk.

Group A: *Can you drink it?*
Group B: *Yes, I can.*

Groups alternate asking and answering questions.
b. Chain Drill (see page 6). Pupils use pictures on page 63 as cues. They should ask *Can you (drink) it?* questions.

EXTENSION

1. Repeat practice from **5a**, printing words *wash, cut,* and *pour* next to food drawings. Teacher points to *chicken* drawing and to word *pour.*

Group A: *Can you pour it?*
Group B: *No, I can't.*

Groups alternate asking and answering questions.

2. Divide class into teams. Use simple board drawings of food and of a boy and a girl (or use magazine pictures of boy and girl) to cue teams. One pupil from each team in turn makes a sentence using correct pronoun, verb in present continuous, and name of food with *a* or *some.* For example, teacher points to picture of girl and pizza. P1: *She's eating some pizza.*

WORKBOOK page 69

- Pupils trace sentences. Then they write sentences to describe last two pictures in sequence. (**Answers**: *I'm pouring it. I'm drinking it.*)
- Pupils trace sentences. Then they draw a line from each sentence to matching picture.
- Pupils circle correct word next to each picture. (**Answers**: *yes, yes, yes, no.*)

Let's Listen

LANGUAGE PATTERNS: Unit review

VOCABULARY: Unit review

MATERIALS: beanbag or ball; tape-recorder and cassette

REVIEW

1. Let's Talk.
Sing 'Peaches, Apples, and Plums' with whole class. Sing it again, with individual pupils substituting different foods, using pictures on PB page 63 as cues.
All: *Peaches, apples, and plums,*
Peaches, apples, and plums.
What do you want?
P1: *I want some (pizza).*
All: *Peaches, apples, and plums.*
Then all say: *I'm (hungry). I want some (pizza).*

2. Let's Learn.
Beanbag Game. Pupils form circle (or remain seated). P1 tosses beanbag to P2.

P1: *What do you want?*
P2: *I want (some apples).* (Tosses beanbag to P3.) *What do you want?*

3. Let's Learn Some More.
Chain Drill (see page 6). Pupils practise question and answer pattern as quickly as possible. P1: *Do you want (some ice cream)?* P2: *Yes, I do.* Pupils use pictures on page 63 as cues, referring to them in order.

4. Let's Move.
a. Charades (see page 6). Whisper sentences from PB page 66 to cue pupils or let them look at book.
b. Robot. Two pupils come to front of class. One tells the other (the robot) how to eat an apple or how to drink juice. The robot should follow the steps exactly, even if incorrect. Class can check their instructions by comparing the robot's actions with pictures on page 66. Continue with other pairs.

PRESENTATION

Teach pupils how to do test. Draw *bread* and *ice cream* on board. Ask one pupil to stand next to board. Make a statement about one of the drawings.

T: *I want some bread.*

Pupil points to correct drawing and teacher ticks board above drawing.

NOTE: If you want to conduct this as a formal test, go immediately to Step **1b** in Open Your Books.

OPEN YOUR BOOKS

1. Pupils open their books to page 67.
a. Play cassette. Pupils listen and point to correct picture.

1. *I'm hungry.*
   What do you want?
   I want some ice cream.
2. *I'm thirsty.*
   What do you want?
   I want some juice.
3. *What do you want?*
   I want some fish and some rice.
4. *What do you want?*
   I want some cake and some ice cream.
5. *Do you want some pizza?*
   Yes, I do.
6. *Do you want some bread?*
   No, I don't. I want some rice.
7. *Can you eat it?*
   Yes, I can.
8. *Can you drink it?*
   No, I can't.

b. Play cassette again. Each pupil does exercise as a written test.

2. Correct tests with pupils.

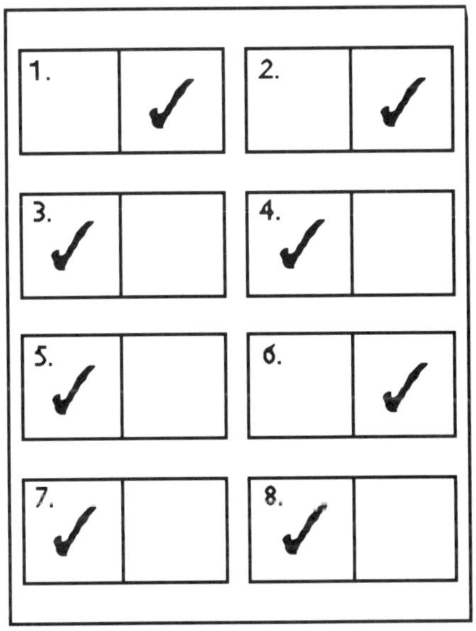

EXTENSION

1. Crazy Picture Dictation (see page 7). Teacher tells pupils to draw pictures, using adjectives, prepositions, and vocabulary from Unit 7, plus any previous vocabulary to be reviewed. The combination of words should result in pictures that are comical but not too difficult for children to draw.

T: *Draw a big apple. On the apple, draw a long fish. By the fish draw a table. On the table draw a bicycle,* etc.

After pupils finish, they compare drawings. (Pupil volunteers can be used to give instructions.)

WORKBOOK page 70

- Pupils write name of each item in blank to complete sentences. (**Answers**: *some ice cream, some milk, some chicken.*)
- Pupils circle answer of their choice next to each picture. Then they write this answer under question. Then they practise question and answer pattern.

Unit Eight

Let's Talk

LANGUAGE PATTERNS: What's your favourite colour? I like (red). What do you like?

NEW VOCABULARY: favourite

MATERIALS: squares of coloured paper (as for Unit 2) or coloured objects; two puppets or soft toys; tape-recorder and cassette

REVIEW

1. Sing 'Peaches, Apples, and Plums'. Divide class into two groups. All: *Peaches, apples, and plums.* Group A: *What do you want?* Group B: *I want an apple.*

2. Substitution Drill (see page 6). Show pupils colour squares (from Unit 2) or various coloured objects (yellow, blue, white, pink, grey, brown, red, black, green, purple, orange). T: *What colour is this?* Ps: *It's (red).*

PRESENTATION

1. Present pattern.
a. Use puppets to model question and answer. Display coloured squares/objects. Puppets look at these.

Puppet A: *What's your favourite colour?*
Puppet B: *Red.*

b. Pupils repeat each line of dialogue three times, in chorus.

2. Practise.
a. Divide class into two groups. Use coloured squares/objects to cue groups.

Group A: *What's your favourite colour?*
Group B: *(Red).*

Groups alternate asking and answering question.
b. Chain Drill (see page 6).

P1: *What's your favourite colour?*
P2: *(Red).* To P3: *What's your favourite colour?*

3. Present complete dialogue.
a. Using puppets, repeat first part of dialogue and add second question and answer.

Puppet A: *What's your favourite colour?*
Puppet B: *Red. What do you like?*
Puppet A: *I like blue.*

b. Pupils repeat each line of dialogue three times, in chorus.

4. Practise.
Divide class into two groups. Use coloured squares/objects to cue groups.

Group A: *What's your favourite colour?*
Group B: *(Red). What do you like?*
Group A: *I like (blue).*

Repeat so that each group practises both parts of dialogue.

OPEN YOUR BOOKS

Open your Pupil's Book to page 68. Show it to pupils and ask them to name the characters.

1. Pupils open their books to page 68.
a. Play cassette. Pupils listen and point to character who is speaking.

Jenny: *What's your favourite colour?*
Andy: *Red. What do you like?*
Jenny: *I like blue.*

b. Play cassette again, stopping after each line. Pupils repeat line.

2. Present sample structure and contraction.
a. Write structure on board. Read it aloud, pointing to words. Pupils repeat.
b. Write explanation of contraction on board: *What is = What's.*
c. Pupils practise *What is your favourite colour?* and *What's your favourite colour?*

3. Practise.
In pairs, pupils practise dialogue using their own favourite colours.

EXTENSION

1. Give each pupil a coloured square or object. Say *I like (red) and (blue).* Pupils with squares/objects in those colours hold them up. As practice continues, increase pace.

2. Treasure Hunt (see page 7). Divide class into pairs. Give class a verbal list of objects to find in the classroom (a red book, a yellow pencil, etc.). Keep list short enough to be remembered (three or four objects). Each pair must 'hunt' for these objects by looking round classroom while remaining seated: when they have found all objects, they put their hands up. When all pairs are ready, ask pupil volunteers to tell class the location of each object. Class repeats location in a full sentence. Ps: *The red book is under the desk. The yellow pencil is on the chair,* etc.

WORKBOOK page 71

- Pupils name the characters. Then they trace words in speech bubbles. Then they complete sentences with colours of their choice and colour each character's shirt. Then they practise question and answer pattern.
- Pupils colour cat's shirt pink. Then they colour shirt held by cat in colour of their choice and write name of colour in blank to complete sentence.

Let's Sing

LANGUAGE PATTERNS: I like (yellow), yes I do. I do, too.

VOCABULARY: Unit review

MATERIALS: multiple classroom objects for Units 1 and 3 vocabulary; squares of coloured paper (several of each); two puppets or soft toys; tape-recorder and cassette

REVIEW

1. Put multiples of classroom objects (from Units 1 and 3) on table. Pupils come up in turn and pick up correct objects.
T: *I like (pencils).* P1 picks up pencils and holds them up for class to see. When all objects have been named, repeat practice with board drawings of flowers, trees, clouds, puddles, and food items (from Unit 7). This time pupils come up in pairs. One pupil says sentence and the other points to correct drawing.

2. Display coloured squares, including yellow, blue, white, pink, grey, brown, red, black, green, purple, and orange. Do a **Chain Drill** (see page 6).

P1: *What's your favourite colour?*
P2: *I like (blue). What do you like?*
P1: *I like (green).*
P2 to P3: *What's your favourite colour?*

Continue.

PRESENTATION

1. Present pattern.
a. Use puppets to model pattern. Place a yellow square on board rail and near it draw an ice cream and a tennis racket. Puppet A touches yellow card.

Puppet A: *I like yellow, yes I do.*
Puppet B: *I do, too.*

b. Pupils repeat each line of dialogue three times, in chorus.
c. Follow Steps **a** and **b** for second and third verses. Puppet touches drawing each time.

2. Practise.
a. Divide class into two groups and chant the song. Clap your hands to keep the beat.

Group A: *I like yellow, yes I do.*
I like yellow, yes I do.
I like yellow.
Group B: *I do, too.*
I like yellow, too.

Continue with *I like ice cream* and *I like tennis.*
Groups alternate for each verse so that each group practises all of the lines.
b. In pairs, pupils practise pattern using **Conversation Lines** (see page 6).

P1: *I like yellow, yes I do.*
P2: *I do, too.*

OPEN YOUR BOOKS

Open your Pupil's Book to page 69 and show it to pupils. Ask them to name the characters and as many of the objects as possible.

1. Pupils open their books to page 69.
a. Play cassette. Pupils listen and point to appropriate colour or object.

I like yellow, yes I do.
I like yellow, yes I do.
I like yellow.
I do, too.
I like yellow, too.

Continue with *I like ice cream* and *I like tennis.*
b. Play cassette again. Pupils sing along.

2. Practise.
a. Sing the song in two groups.

Group A: *I like (yellow), yes I do.*
I like yellow, yes I do.
I like yellow.
Group B: *I do, too.*
I like yellow, too.

Repeat for verses 2 and 3.

b. Divide class into three groups and assign one verse to each group. The group stands to sing *I like (ice cream), yes I do.* The whole class sings *I do, too. I like (ice cream), too.*

EXTENSION

1. Chain Drill (see page 6). Use squares of coloured paper (several of each). Give each pupil a square. (P1 has red square.) P1: *I like red.* To P2: *What do you like?* If P2 also has red square, he/she answers: *I like red, too.* P2 to P3: *What do you like?* If P2 does not have a red square, he/she answers: *I like (yellow).* Continue.

2. Memory Chain (see page 7). Divide class into two or three teams. In turn, each team tries to make chain as long as possible without forgetting any items. Each pupil in team adds one item to chain of likes.

P1: *I like (clouds).*
P2: *I like (clouds) and (rabbits).*
P3: *I like (clouds) and (rabbits) and (rice).*

Let's Learn

LANGUAGE PATTERNS: Look! There's (a dog). What do you like? I like (frogs), too.

NEW VOCABULARY: a dog, dogs, a frog, frogs, (a cat), cats, a spider, spiders, a bird, birds, a rabbit, rabbits

MATERIALS: multiple classroom objects for Units 1 and 3 vocabulary; magazine pictures of new animal words listed above; two puppets or soft toys; tape-recorder and cassette

REVIEW

1. Divide class into two groups and sing 'What Do You Like?'

Group A: *I like (yellow), yes I do.*
I like (yellow), yes I do.
I like (yellow).
Group B: *I do, too.*
I like (yellow), too.

Sing the song twice, so that each group sings both parts.

2. Substitution Drill (see page 6). Drill pattern *I like (flowers)* using multiples of classroom objects (from Units 1 and 3) and simple board drawings of multiple objects from Units 6 and 7 to cue pupils.

PRESENTATION

1. Present new vocabulary.
a. Use magazine pictures or simple board drawings of animals to introduce new words, one at a time. Pupils repeat several times. After each new word, conduct a quick mini-drill, alternating new word with previously introduced words.
b. Drill new vocabulary, emphasizing difference between singular and plural.

T: *A (dog).* Ps: *A (dog).*
T: *(Dogs).* Ps: *(Dogs).*

2. Present pattern.
a. Place magazine pictures on board rail or use simple board drawings of new animal words. Use puppets to model pattern. Puppet A points to picture of dog, for example.

Puppet A: *Look! There's a dog. I like dogs.*

b. Pupils repeat three times, in chorus.

3. Practise.
Divide class into two groups. Use magazine pictures or simple board drawings of new animal words to cue groups.

Group A: *Look! There's (a dog).*
Group B: *I like (dogs).*

4. Present question and answer pattern.
a. Use puppets to model question and answer. Puppets look at magazine pictures/board drawings.

Puppet A: *What do you like?*
Puppet B: *I like (frogs).*
Puppet A: *I like (frogs), too.*

b. Pupils repeat each line of dialogue three times, in chorus.

5. Practise.
a. Divide class into two groups. Use magazine pictures/board drawings of new animal words to cue groups.
b. Chain Drill (see page 6).

P1: *What do you like?*
P2: *I like (birds).*
P1: *I like (birds), too.*

P2: *What do you like?*
P3: *I like (spiders).*
P2: *I like (spiders), too.*

Continue.

OPEN YOUR BOOKS

Open your Pupil's Book to page 70 and show it to pupils. Ask them to name the characters and to say what each child in lower picture is holding. (**Answers**: *a dog, a frog, frogs.*)

1. Pupils open their books to page 70.
a. Play cassette. Pupils listen and point to character who is speaking.

John: *Look! There's a dog. I like dogs. What do you like?*
Jenny: *I like frogs.*
Andy: *I like frogs, too.*

b. Play cassette again, stopping after each line. Pupils repeat line.

2. Present sample structures. Write structures on board. Read them aloud, pointing to words. Pupils repeat words.

3. Practise.
a. Divide class into two groups. Practise question and answer pattern with new vocabulary on PB page 71, using cats as models.
b. In pairs, pupils continue question and answer practice.

4. Look at activity at bottom of page 71.
a. In pairs, pupils look at pictures of toy animals. Pupils take turns asking and answering questions about the toys.

P1: *What do you like?*
P2: *I like (spiders).*
P1: *I like (spiders), too.*

b. Repeat activity. Pupils select two toys and form a sentence using *and.*

P1: *What do you like?*
P2: *I like (spiders) and (dogs).*
P1: *I like (spiders) and (dogs), too.*

(Continued on page 79.)

EXTENSION

1. Ask a pupil volunteer to come to front. Use magazine pictures/simple board drawings of new animal words to cue volunteer. Assign animal names to six pupils. Volunteer chooses picture, points to it, and says: *Look! There's (a dog).* Pupil assigned dog comes forward. All: *I like (dogs).* Repeat for all animals.

2. Charades (see page 6). Divide class into two teams. Give P1 from Team A the part of a (cat) to act out. Team B guesses, saying: *I like (cats). What do you like?* Team B answers: *I like (cats), too.* Repeat for other animals, giving all pupils a chance to act animal part. Award points for correct guesses.

WORKBOOK pages 72 and 73

page 72

- Pupils draw a line from each picture to correct name. Then they trace names.
- Pupils draw animals of their choice in box and write names in blank to complete sentence.

page 73

- Pupils draw a line from each question to appropriate answer. (**Answers**: *What's your favourite colour? Red. / What do you want? I want some ice cream. / What's he doing? He's climbing a tree. / Where are the apples? They're on the tree. / How many plums are there? There's one. / What are you doing? I'm playing tag.*)
- Pupils trace sentence. Then they write a sentence with the name of their choice from each pair of pictures.
- Pupils trace sentences. Then they write two sentences for each picture. (**Answers**: *There's an apple. I like apples. / There's a robot. I like robots. / There's a bicycle. I like bicycles.*)

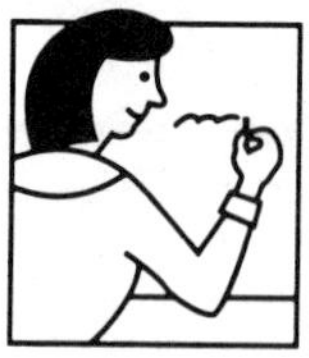

Let's Learn Some More

LANGUAGE PATTERNS: Do you like (rabbits)? Yes, I do. No, I don't.

VOCABULARY: General review

MATERIALS: classroom objects for Units 1 and 3 vocabulary; magazine pictures of birds, dogs, cats, rabbits, frogs, and spiders; two puppets or soft toys; tape-recorder, *Let's Speak English* cassette, and music cassette; grids (one for each pupil) with three numbered squares; two slips of paper marked with tick and cross

REVIEW

1. Use classroom objects to review vocabulary from Units 1 and 3. Teacher or pupil volunteer says: *There's (a pen).* Pupils hold up or point to appropriate object. Ps: *I like (pens).*

2. Chain Drill (see page 6). Review names of animals from Let's Learn. Pupils can use pictures on PB page 71 as cues.

P1: *What do you like?*
P2: *I like (rabbits). What do you like?*
P3: *I like (birds). What do you like?*

PRESENTATION

1. Present question and affirmative answer pattern.

a. Make multiple board drawings of birds, dogs, cats, rabbits, frogs, and spiders or use magazine pictures. Use puppets to model question and answer pattern. Puppet A points to picture of rabbits.

Puppet A: *Do you like rabbits?*
Puppet B: *Yes, I do.*

b. Pupils repeat each line of dialogue three times, in chorus.

2. Practise.

a. Divide class into two groups. Drill the pattern using board drawings/ magazine pictures of animals to cue groups.

Group A: *Do you like (rabbits)?*
Group B: *Yes, I do.*

Groups alternate asking and answering question.
b. In pairs, pupils continue to practise pattern. Pupils can use pictures on PB page 71 as cues.

3. Present negative answer pattern.

a. Puppet B points to drawing/ magazine picture of spiders as teacher models question and answer.

Puppet B: *Do you like spiders?*
Puppet A: *No, I don't.*

b. Pupils repeat each line of dialogue three times, in chorus.

4. Practise.

a. Divide class into two groups. Using board drawings/magazine pictures of animals as before, cue groups by pointing to a picture and either nodding (yes) or shaking your head (no).

T: *Do you like (spiders)?* (no)
Group A: *No, I don't.*

Continue with Group B.

b. Chain Drill (see page 6). Pupils can use pictures on page 71 as cues.

P1: *Do you like (cats)?*
P2: *Yes, I do. Do you like (rabbits)?*
P3: *No, I don't.*

Continue.

OPEN YOUR BOOKS

Open your Pupil's Book to page 72. Show it to pupils and ask them to name the characters. (Option: Pupils say, in own language, what they think each picture is about.)

1. Pupils open their books to page 72.

a. Play cassette. Pupils listen and point to character who is speaking.

John: *Do you like rabbits?*
Jenny: *Yes, I do.*
Andy: *Do you like spiders?*
John: *No, I don't.*

b. Play cassette again, stopping after each line. Pupils repeat line.

2. Present sample structures and contraction.

a. Write structures on board. Read them aloud, pointing to words. Pupils repeat.
b. Write explanation of contraction on board: *do not = don't.*
c. Pupils practise saying *No, I do not* and *No, I don't.*

3. Practise.
Look at activity at top of PB page 73.

a. Model question and answer presented by cats. Pupils repeat.
b. Ask individual pupils *Do you like (robots)?* Pupils can answer either *No, I don't* or *Yes, I do,* according to their personal preferences. Ask as many pupils as possible. Continue with other picture cues.
c. In pairs, pupils practise asking and answering questions, following cats' model and using picture cues.

EXTENSION

1. Pass the Puppet (see page 7). Use board drawings/magazine pictures of animals and two slips of paper, one with a tick and one with a cross. Play music as pupils pass a puppet or soft toy around. When music stops, offer slips of paper, face down, to pupil holding puppet. Pupil selects slip. Then point to an animal picture. Ps: *Do you like (rabbits)?* P1: *Yes, I do* or *No, I don't* (depending on whether paper has tick or cross). Pupil can pretend to speak as puppet.

(Continued on page 81.)

2. Number Grid (see page 7). Give each pupil a grid with three numbered squares. Pupils draw an animal in each square, using pictures on PB page 71 to help them if necessary.

T: *Number 1.*
P1: (Looks at own drawings.) *There's a (rabbit) in number 1.*
P2: (Looks at own drawings.) *Yes, there is* or *No, there isn't. There's a (spider) in number 1.*

Continue with other pupils and then repeat for squares 2 and 3.

WORKBOOK page 74

NOTE: There is only one Workbook page for this activity; Let's Move has an extra Workbook page.

- Pupils trace answer under each picture.
- Pupils write either *Yes, I do* or *No, I don't* under each picture. Then they practise question and answer pattern.

Let's Learn the Alphabet

NEW VOCABULARY: window, x-ray, zero

MATERIALS: tape-recorder and cassette; lined paper

1. Review alphabet by singing 'The Alphabet Song'.

2. Pupils open their books to bottom of page 73.

a. Play cassette. Pupils listen and point to letters.

Teacher: *W, window; X, x-ray; Y, yo-yo; Z, zero.*

b. Play cassette again, stopping after each letter. Pupils repeat letter and word.

c. Say word *window* carefully, emphasizing initial sound. Print word *window* on board and underline *w*.

d. Print letter *w* next to word *window* on board.

w—window

Ask pupils to think of other words that begin with the same sound (e.g. *wind*).

e. Repeat Steps **c** and **d** for words *x-ray, yo-yo,* and *zero.*

3. Show pupils how to print a small *w*. Then introduce capital *W*. Repeat for letters *X, Y,* and *Z.* Practise printing letters on lined paper.

WORKBOOK page 75

- Pupils draw a line from each letter to correct picture. Then they trace words.
- Pupils trace words in balloons. Then they draw a line from each child to balloon with the word that begins with letter on child's shirt.

Let's Move

LANGUAGE PATTERNS: I'm (walking)/(running)/(swimming)/(flying)/(hopping)/(jumping). Can it (run)? Yes, it can. No, it cannot.

NEW VOCABULARY: walking, run(ning), swim(ming), fly(ing), hop(ping), jumping

MATERIALS: tape-recorder and cassette

REVIEW

1. Charades (see page 6). Use four pupil volunteers to act out 'juice' and 'apple' sequences. Use pictures on PB page 66 to cue them. P1 acts out buying juice. Class guesses. Ps: *I'm buying some juice.*

2. Chain Drill (see page 6). Pupils use pictures on PB page 71 as prompts.

P1: *Do you like (rabbits)?*
P2: *Yes, I do./ No, I don't. Do you like (frogs)?*
P3: *Yes, I do./No, I don't. Do you like (cats)?*

PRESENTATION

1. Present action sentences.
   a. Model sentences using clear gestures.
   b. Say sentences. Pupils listen and repeat.
   c. Use six pupil volunteers. Volunteers come to front. Give each a sentence to act out. Class then repeats sentence.

2. Play a game.
Divide class into two groups and play **Charades** (see page 6). Whisper sentences to cue actors.

OPEN YOUR BOOKS

Open your Pupil's Book to page 74 and show it to pupils. Point to each picture in turn and say sentence. Pupils repeat sentence.

1. Pupils open their books to page 74.
   a. Play cassette. Pupils listen and point to each action.

   I'm walking.
   I'm running.
   I'm swimming.
   I'm flying.
   I'm hopping.
   I'm jumping.

   b. Play cassette again, stopping after each sentence. Pupils repeat sentence.

2. Say sentences in random order. Pupils point to correct pictures and repeat sentences.

3. Ask pupils, one at a time, to point to a picture and say sentence (with teacher's help). Class repeats sentence while a pupil volunteer mimes action.

4. Present sample structures and contraction.
   a. Write structures on board. Read them aloud, pointing to words. Pupils repeat.
   b. Write explanation of contraction on board: *cannot = can't.*
   c. Pupils practise saying *No, it cannot* and *No, it can't.*
   d. In pairs, pupils practise question and answer pattern for questions at bottom of page 74.

EXTENSION

1. Guessing Game (see page 6). One pupil opens book to page 71 and decides on an animal. Individual pupils ask questions to find out name of animal. P1 chooses animal. P2: *Can it (fly)?* P1: *Yes, it can* or *No, it can't.* When class has guessed correctly, P1 chooses any one action that can be performed by his/her animal and does/mimes it. Class guesses, saying: *(She's) (swimming).*

WORKBOOK pages 76 and 77

NOTE: There are two Workbook pages for this activity in order to give pupils extra practice in using the present continuous.

page 76
- Pupils trace words. Then they draw a line from each sentence to matching picture.
- Pupils trace answers under pictures.
- Pupils write answers under pictures. (**Answers**: *Yes, it can. No, it cannot.*) Then they practise question and answer pattern.

page 77
- Pupils trace words. Then they write sentences for three pictures, using present continuous. (**Answers**: *I'm hopping. I'm running. I'm jumping.* **NOTE**: *He's running*, etc. is also acceptable.)
- Pupils trace sentences. Then they draw a line from each sentence to matching picture.
- Pupils circle correct answer next to each sentence. (**Answers**: *Yes, Yes, No, No.*)

Let's Listen

LANGUAGE PATTERNS: Unit review
VOCABULARY: Unit review
MATERIALS: one puppet or soft toy; tape-recorder and cassette

REVIEW

1. Let's Talk.
Pass the Puppet (see page 7) Play the song 'What do you like?' while pupils pass a puppet to each other. When music stops, class asks pupil holding puppet: *What's your favourite colour?* P1: (*Red*). To puppet: *What do you like?* Pupil to right of P1 answers for puppet. P2: *I like (blue).*

2. Let's Learn.
Do simple board drawings of single and multiple animals. Point to drawings at random. Ps: *A bird* or *Birds.*

3. Let's Learn Some More.
Divide class into two teams. To cue teams, draw simple animals (in multiples) as well as a tick and a cross. Teacher points to drawing of (dogs). Team A: *Do you like (dogs)?* Teacher points to cross. Team B: *No, I don't.* Award points for correct questions and answers.

4. Let's Move.
Guessing Game (see page 6). Divide class into two teams. Assign an animal to P1 from Team A. (Show P1 picture of animal on PB page 71 but do not let rest of class see.) The other pupils try to guess animal by asking questions. They can use pictures on PB page 74 as cues.

P2: *Can it walk?*
P1: *Yes, it can.*
P3: *Can it run?*
P1: *Yes, it can.*
P4: *Can it hop?*
P1: *No, it can't.*
P4: *Is it a dog?*
P1: *Yes, it is.*

PRESENTATION

Teach pupils how to do test. Draw two cats and two dogs on board. Ask one pupil to stand next to board. Make a statement about one of the drawings.

T: *I like (dogs).*

Pupil points to correct drawing and teacher ticks board above drawing.

NOTE: If you want to conduct this as a formal test, go immediately to Step **1b** in Open Your Books.

OPEN YOUR BOOKS

1. Pupils open their books to page 75.
a. Play cassette. Pupils listen and point to correct picture.

1. *What's your favourite colour?*
   Green. What do you like?
   I like blue.
2. *What's your favourite colour?*
   Yellow. What do you like?
   I like purple.
3. *What do you like?*
   I like frogs.
4. *What do you like?*
   I like cats.
5. *Do you like spiders?*
   No, I don't.
6. *Do you like rabbits?*
   Yes, I do.
7. *Can it fly?*
   Yes, it can.
8. *Can it walk?*
   No, it can't.

b. Play cassette again. Each pupil does exercise as a written test.

2. Correct tests with pupils.

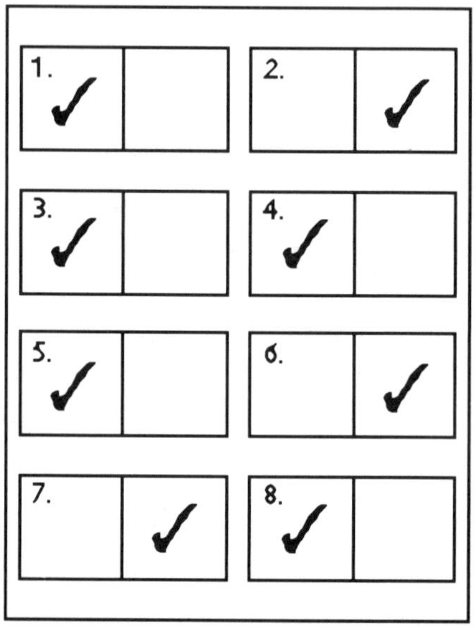

EXTENSION

1. Make simple board drawings of animals. Divide class into two teams. Call out name of animal. P1 from Team A comes to front, points to correct picture, and says: *Look! There's (a dog). I like (dogs).*
P1 then turns to P2 from same team and completes second part of dialogue.

P1: *What do you like?*
P2: *I like (frogs).*
P1: *I like (frogs), too.*

Teams earn one point for each part of dialogue completed correctly.

WORKBOOK page 78

- Pupils write correct word in each blank to complete sentence. (**Answers**: *a bird, a dog.*)
- Pupils circle answer of their choice next to each picture. Then they trace words. Then they write their choice in blank to complete each sentence.
- Pupils circle answer of their choice next to each picture. Then they write answer under picture. Then they practise question and answer pattern.

Let's Review

LANGUAGE PATTERNS: General review

VOCABULARY: General review

MATERIALS: beanbag or ball; sets of dice; squares of coloured paper (as for Unit 2); tape-recorder and cassette; magazine pictures or realia of animals, toys, and food

REVIEW

1. Songs.

a. Sing 'Peaches, Apples, and Plums' and 'What Do You Like?'

b. Pupils get into **Conversation Lines** (see page 6). P1: *What's your favourite colour?* P2: *(Red).*

2. Vocabulary.

Beanbag Game (see page 6). Pupils stand in a circle (or remain seated). P1 tosses beanbag or ball to P2. P1: *I'm (hungry)* or *I'm (thirsty).* P2: *What do you want? P1: I want (some ice cream).* Continue activity until all pupils have asked and answered question.

3. Structures.

a. Play Restaurant in small groups. Use pictures on PB page 64 as cues. Each pupil has a turn to be waiter. Model activity for class.

P1 (Waiter): *What do you want?*
P2: *I want (some ice cream).*
P3: *I want (some chicken) and (some rice).*
P1: *Do you want (some milk)?*
P2: *Yes, I do* or *No, I don't.*

Then, P1 should pretend to serve and P2 pretend to eat food.

P1: *Here you are.*
P2: *Thank you.*
P1: *You're welcome.*

b. Use simple board drawings of animals and squares of coloured paper. In pairs, pupils come up to front.

P1: *What do you like?* (Points to drawing of (frog).)
P2: *I like (frogs).* (Points to drawing of (rabbit).) Do you like (rabbits)?
P1: *Yes, I do* or *No, I don't.*
Then teacher holds up coloured square. All: *I like (red) (frogs), and (red) (rabbits).*

4. Action sentences.

a. Give actions from PB page 66, in random order, to eight pupils, one action per pupil. Pupils must arrange themselves in correct logical order and then say the sentences.

b. Quickly review movement sentences from Unit 8. Then point to animal pictures on PB page 71, one at a time, and ask pupils the following. T: *Can it (hop)?* Class responds. Ps: *Yes, it can* or *No, it can't.*

OPEN YOUR BOOKS

1. Say these.

Pupils open their books to page 76. Teacher circulates as pupils do the following activities.

a. Pupils review vocabulary by pointing to each picture in order and calling out name of picture in chorus. (**Answers**: *a big dog, a little spider, a little rabbit, a big frog, a little cat, a big spider, a big cat, a little dog, a big rabbit, a little frog.*)

b. Divide class into pairs. Give each pair a dice. Pupils take turns rolling the dice, moving number of spaces equal to number on dice, and identifying picture. Pupils continue game until one pupil lands directly on goal.

c. Divide class into pairs. P1 identifies all picture cues as quickly as possible. P2 listens and helps P1 if necessary. If all pictures are identified correctly, P1 receives 10 points. Reverse roles and play again.

2. Answer the question.

Divide class into two groups. Group A asks Group B: *What do you want?* Group B answers: *I want some (bread).* Continue for each item in picture, reversing roles.

3. Say and act.

a. Look at pictures at top of PB page 77. Point to speech bubble in first picture and say *Here you are.* Point to blank speech bubbles and ask pupils to guess what should be there. (**Answers**: *Thank you. You're welcome.*) Repeat for second picture. (**Answer**: *What's your favourite colour?*)

b. In pairs, pupils practisé dialogues. Teacher should circulate, helping as necessary.

4. Ask your partner.

In pairs, pupils interview each other using picture cues on questionnaire. P1: *Do you like (pink)?* P2: *Yes, I do* or *No, I don't.* Pupils should tick either *Yes* or *No* after each question to match their partner's answers. Each pupil asks and answers questions. Teacher should circulate, helping as necessary.

5. Listen carefully.

a. Play cassette. Pupils listen and point to correct picture.

a: *Can it run?*
No, it can't.
b: *Can it swim?*
Yes, it can.

b. Play cassette again. Pupils listen and tick small box next to correct answer.

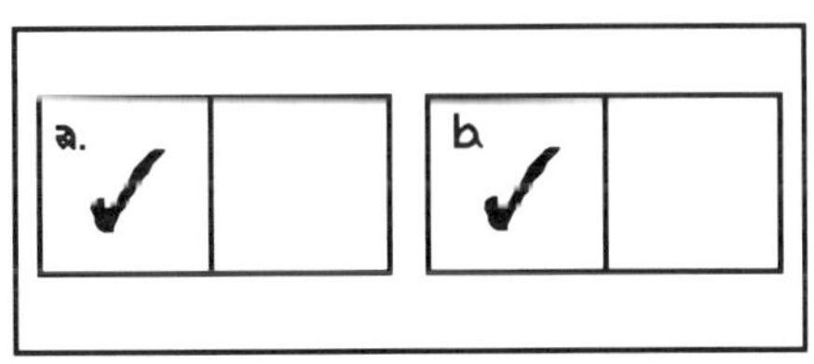

c. Pupils identify other two pictures.

(Continued on page 86.)

EXTENSION

1. I See Something. Teach pupils the phrase *I see something.* Use realia, magazine pictures, and board drawings of animals, food, and toys. One pupil secretly chooses an object and says *I see something.* The other pupils in the group try to guess what card it is by asking questions like *Is it red? Is it big? Can it run?,* etc.

WORKBOOK pages 79 and 80

page 79

- Pupils complete crossword by filling in name of each object (one letter per square). (**Answers**: **Down** 1 *doll,* 2 *eraser,* 3 *brother,* 4 *dog,* 6 *zero,* 8 *yoyo,* 9 *marker,* 10 *house,* 12 *octopus,* 13 *boy,* 16 *spider,* 18 *nine.* **Across** 3 *bird,* 5 *girl,* 7 *cassette,* 9 *mother,* 11 *robot,* 14 *ink,* 15 *desk,* 17 *pencil,* 19 *car,* 20 *sun,* 21 *xray.*)

page 80

- Pupils trace word. Then they unscramble other words and write them in blanks. (**Answers**: *birds, frogs, cats.*) Then they draw a line from each group of animals to its name.
- Pupils complete sentence with answer of their choice. Then they practise question and answer pattern.
- Pupils follow line from each food item to its sentence. Then they write name of food item in blank. Then they trace words.

Midterm Test

A Write.

1. What's this?

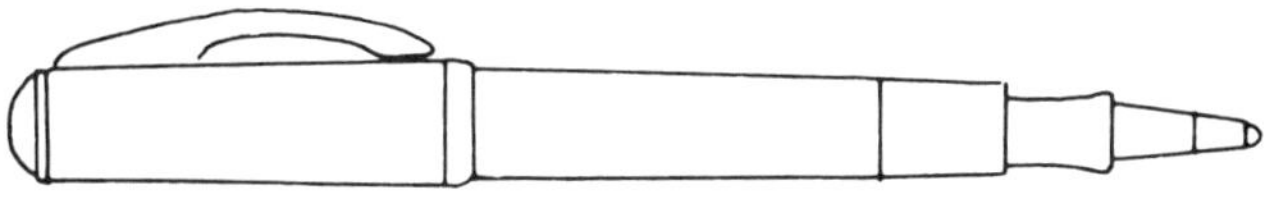

It's a ______.

2. What's this?

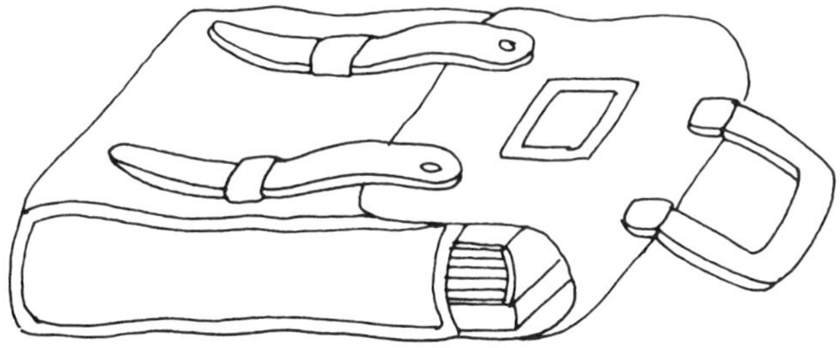

__________ __ ______.

3. What are these?

They're __________.

4. What are these?

______________ ______________.

5.

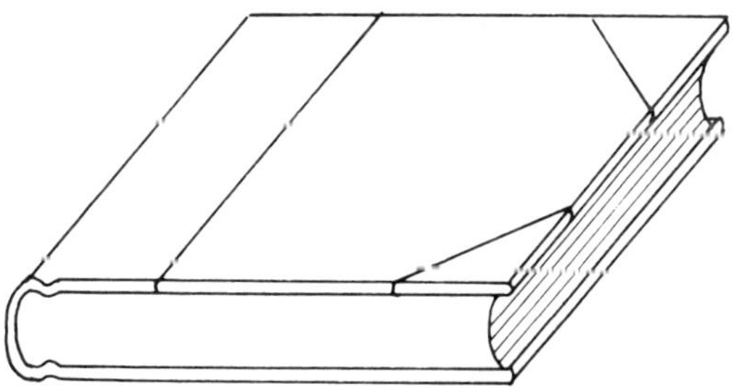

This is a ________.

6.

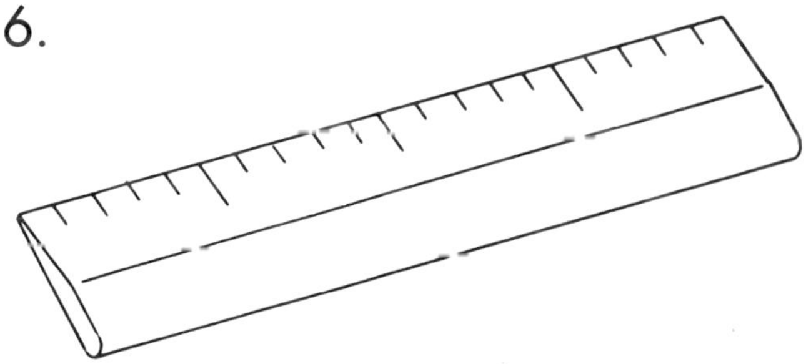

________ ____ __ __________.

7.

These are ______________.

8.

________ _____ ____________.

B Count and write.

How many?

teachers one

boys ______ chairs ______ girls ______ desks ______

C Write.

1.

He's fat.

She's ______.

2.

He's ______.

She's ______.

D Write.

1. Who's she?

______ my ________________.

2. Who's he?

______ my ________________.

E Write.

Look at the board.
Open your book.
Put your book away.
Pick up your pencil.

1.

________ ________ ________.

2.

______ ______ ______ ________.

3.

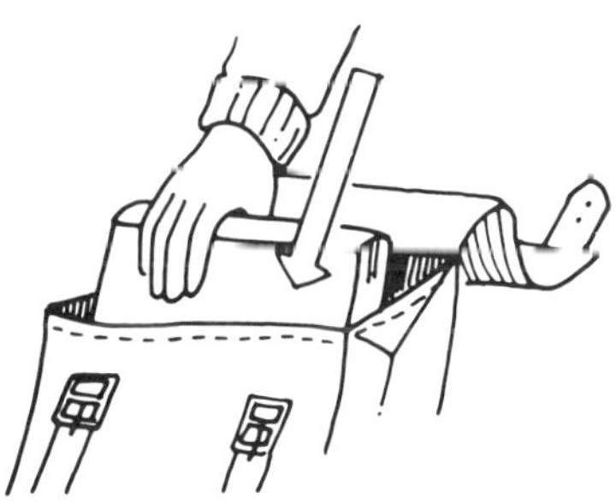

______ ______ ______ ________.

4.

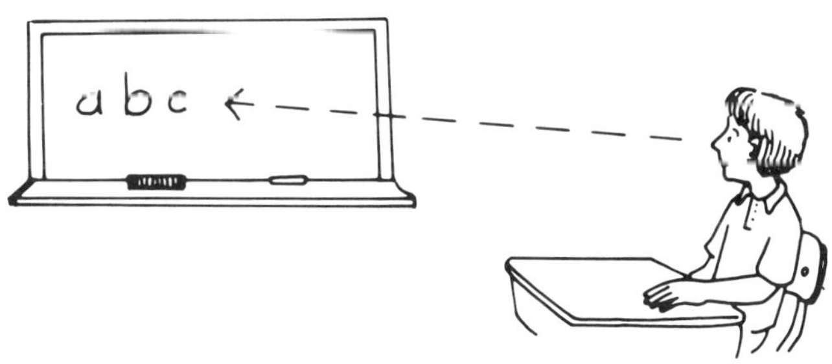

______ ______ ______ ________.

F Write.

1.

2.

G Write the letters.

1. A B __ __ E __ G __
2. L __ __ __ P __ R __

H Join the letters.

D	g
H	b
E	d
J	h
B	j
G	e

Final Test

A Write.

1. What is it?

It's a ________.

2. What is it?

____ __ ______.

B Write.

1. Is it a big robot?

No, ____ ____ ______.
It's a _________ robot.

2. Is it a long skipping rope?

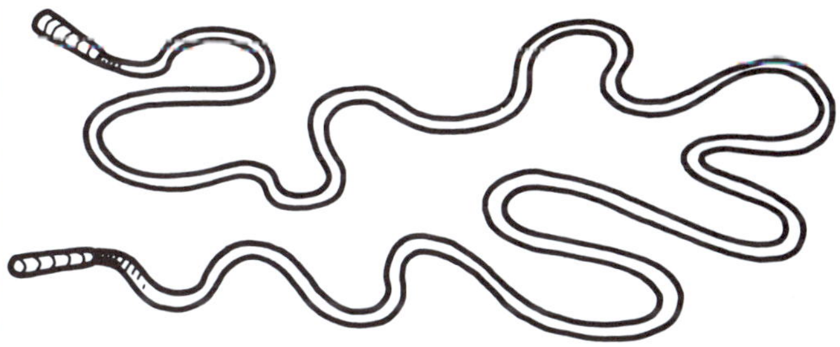

______, ____ ____.

C Count and write.

How many are there?

1. There are two kites.
2. There's ______ cloud.
3. __________ ______ __________flowers.
4. __________ ______ bicycle.

D Write.

1. Where's the pencil?

It's ____ the ________.

2. Where's the dog?

________ _________ _____ _______.

3. Where are the birds?

They're ____ the ________.

4. Where are the spiders?

____________ ___ _____ _______.

E Write.

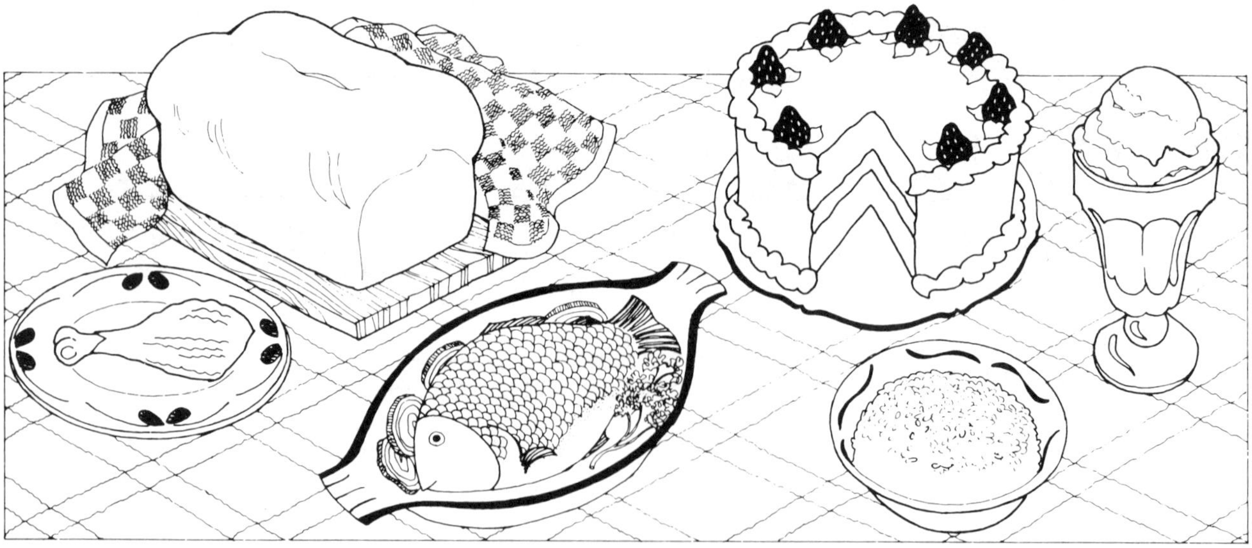

What do you want?

I want __________ __________ and __________ __________.

F Write.

1. Do you like frogs?	2. What do you like?

______, ____ __________.	I like ____________________.

G Write.

1. Can you play with a yo-yo?	2. Can it swim?
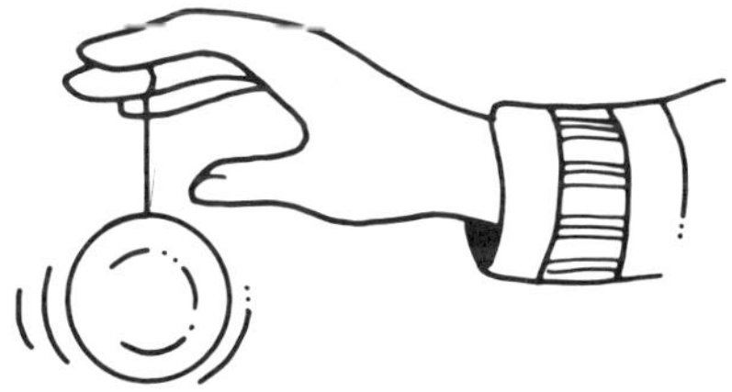	
______, __ __________.	______, ______ ______.

H Write.

1. Is he hitting a ball?	2. Is she riding a bicycle?

______, __ __________.	______, ______ ______.

I Write.

1.

I'm ____________ an apple.

2.

________ ________ it.

3.

______ ____________ it.

4.

______ ____________ _____.

J Write.

1.

2.

Midterm Test Answer Key

A Write.
1. It's a pen.
2. It's a bag.
3. They're desks.
4. They're rackets.
5. This is a book.
6. This is a ruler.
7. These are cassettes.
8. These are markers.

B Count and write.
boys five
chairs seven
girls three
desks eight

C Write.
1. She's thin.
2. He's tall.
   She's short.

D Write.
1. She's my mother.
2. He's my grandfather.

E Write.
1. Open your book.
2. Pick up your pencil.
3. Put your book away.
4. Look at the board.

F Write.
1. Hello! I'm Kate.
   What's your name?
   Hi! My name is John.
2. Hi, Lisa.
   How are you?
   I'm fine, thank you.

G Write the letters.
1. A B C D E F G H
2. L M N O P Q R S

H Join the letters.
D/d, H/h, E/e, J/j, B/b, G/g.

Final Test Answer Key

A Write.
1. It's a kite.
2. It's a car.

B Write.
1. No, it isn't.
   It's a little robot.
2. Yes, it is.

C Count and write.
2. There's one cloud.
3. There are three flowers.
4. There's one bicycle.

D Write.
1. It's on the desk (or table).
2. It's under the tree.
3. They're in the tree.
4. They're by the book.

E Write.
1. (Answers will vary. Pupils must use some.)

F Write.
1. Yes, I do or No, I don't.
2. (Answers will vary.)

G Write.
1. Yes, I can or No, I can't.
2. No, it can't.

H Write.
1. No, he isn't.
2. Yes, she is.

I Write.
1. I'm buying an apple.
2. I'm washing it.
3. I'm cutting it.
4. I'm eating it.

J Write.
1. Here you are.
   Thank you.
   You're welcome.
2. How old are you?
   I'm (seven) years old. (Ages will vary.)

Materials Needed

- name tags/cards—one per pupil
- 3 puppets *OR* soft toys; beanbag *OR* ball; small ball; yo-yo; small doll wrapped in paper; box with toys; sets of dice—one set per pair
- cloth; 2 bags; box; a few coins
- birthday hat *OR* other realia; props to show sunny, rainy, windy, and snowy days (e.g. umbrella, etc)
- glass; carton/bottle of fruit juice
- apple; 2 peaches, 2 apples, 2 plums *OR* magazine pictures *OR* teacher-made cards of these
- classroom objects—several of each: pen, pencil, pencil case, ruler, bag, eraser, cassette, crayon, marker, notebook; a few multi-coloured classroom objects
- photographs of pupils' families
- slips of paper—enough for whole class—half with ticks and half with crosses; 2 teacher-made cards with *is* and *isn't* on them; card with drawing of robot in small box
- lined paper for writing; big sheets of paper for pupils' family trees
- grids with 3 numbered squares and bingo grids—several per pupil
- big squares of paper in red, green, blue, yellow, orange, pink, purple, brown, black, white, grey—3 of each and 6 of red and blue.
- magazine pictures *OR* teacher-made cards of *mother, father, sister, brother, grandfather, grandmother, baby sister*; people who are *tall, short, young, old, pretty, ugly, fat, thin*—several of each; *flower, tree, cloud, puddle*—singles and multiples; *ice cream, milk, chicken, pizza, rice, bread; dog, cat, frog, spider, bird, rabbit*—singles and multiples.

Word List

A

a 8
alphabet 11
am 6
an 9
and 18
apple 19
are 14
at 20
away 20

B

baby 35
bag 9
ball 45
be 12
bicycle 45
big 46
bird 71
birthday 42
black 17
blowing 51
blue 17
board 20
book 9
box 46
boy 30
bread 63
brother 33
brown 17
buying 66
by 54

C

cake 62
can 48
cannot 48
can't 48
car 45
carefully 12
cassette 26
cat 8
catch 48
chair 9
chicken 63
circle 30
climbing 56
close 12
cloud 52
colour 16
come 30
count 30
crayon 27
cutting 66

D

day 51
desk 9
dinner 38
do 38
dog 70
doll 44
don't 38
door 30
down 12
draw 30
drink 66
drinking 66

E

eat 38
eating 66
egg 29
eight 28
English 11
eraser 9

F

family 33
fat 36
father 33
favourite 68
fine 14
fish 29
five 28
flower 53
fly 74
flying 56
for 42
four 28
friend 24
frog 70

G

girl 30
give 30
go out 51
go to 30
good morning 38
good night 38
grandfather 34
grandmother 34
grey 17
green 17

H

hand 20
Happy birthday 42
he 34
he's 34
hello 6
here 30
hi 6
hit 48
home 32
homework 38
hop 74
hopping 74
house 37
how 14
hungry 60

I

I 6
ice cream 62
I'm 14
in 54
ink 37
is 6
isn't 10
it 8
it's 8

J

jeans 37
juice 60
jumping 74

K

kick 48
kite 45
know 44

L

let's 24
like 11
line 30
lion 47
listen 12
little 46
long 46
look 20

M

make 30
many 28
marker 27
me 30
meet 32
mess 38
milk 63
mother 32
my 6

N

name 6
nice 32
nine 28
no 10
not 10
notebook 27
now 43

O

octopus 55
oh 51
old 36
on 54
one 28
open 12
opening 66
orange 17
out 20

P

peach 61
pen 9
pencil 9
pencil case 26
piano 38
pick up 20
picture 30
pink 17
pizza 63
play 24
playing 56
please 12
plum 61
point to 12
pouring 66
pretty 36
puddle 53
purple 17
put away 20
put down 20
put up 20
puzzle 45

Q

question 55
quiet 12

R

rabbit 71
racket 45
raining 50
rainy 51
reading 56
red 16
rice 63
riding 56
robot 42
round 46
ruler 8
run 74
running 74

S

seven 28
she 34
she's 34
shining 50
short 36
sister 33
sit down 12
six 28
skip 48
skipping rope 45
sleep 38
snowing 51
snowy 51
some 60
song 7
spider 71
square 46
stand up 12
sun 50
sunny 51
swim 74
swimming 74

T

table 27
tag 56
take out 20
tall 36
teacher 12
ten 28
tennis 56
thank you 14
the 12
there 52
there's 52
these 26
they 26
they're 26
thin 36
thirsty 60
this 8
three 28
tidy up 38
to 12
today 43
too 32
touch 12
trainer 28
tree 53
TV 38
two 28

U

ugly 36
umbrella 65
under 54
up 12

V

van 65

W

wake up 38
walking 74
want 60
washing 66
watch 38
welcome 60
what 6
what's 6
where 54
where's 54
white 17
who 34
who's 34
wind 51
window 73
windy 51
with 48
wow 42
write 20

X

x-ray 73

Y

years 42
yellow 17
yes 10
yo-yo 45
you 14
young 36
your 6
you're 43

Z

zero 73